Living without a Name
A View through Black Eyes

Living without a Name
A View through Black Eyes

by

Ronald J. DeLoach

Lacy —
A man has to live his
Dreams — keep living
yours

9-12-09

DORRANCE PUBLISHING CO., INC.
PITTSBURGH, PENNSYLVANIA 15222

In Tribute to My Father

ISBN: 978-1-4349-0361-7
Printed in the United States of America

First Printing

For more information or to order additional books, please contact:
Dorrance Publishing Co., Inc.
701 Smithfield Street
Pittsburgh, Pennsylvania 15222
U.S.A.
1-800-788-7654

Dedication

To my wife, Veronica, for all your hard work, and to my brother, Randall, for helping me get started and maintain my focus—much love! In addition, Adrian Porter, thanks for helping me with this document. Finally, to Dr. Barbara Dubins of San Jose State University, for peaking my interest in African studies, and to Caitlin Madrigal, for your assistance in editing my manuscript.

CONTENTS

a page for your THOUGHTS

Legacy

Daughter of slave's stresses
In see-through crumpled dresses
A forgotten debt now reflects
As a hateful shadow of the rest
Beauty's blood is driven, and
still the women stroll, unimpressed

The legacy of African people is the struggle to survive. We were once a great people, who built great civilizations. Thousands of years of external assaults on the continent's social growth have led African people to this moment in time. We African Americans are the descendants of the last movement of African people. Some black Americans now participate in the act of holding themselves down for the sake of money. The effects of slavery in America have reached a new high.

Who are black people? Black people, according to Wikipedia, are merely people with dark pigmented skin. Do black people exist as a race? There are black people in Australia, Polynesia, the islands of Southeast Asia, India, the Middle East, the Caribbean, Central and South America, Africa, and Europe. So what makes black people in America different from other black people in the world? I believe the difference is what we cannot remember. A failed memory is the primary reason we refer to ourselves as a color. We have been forgetting the spirit of our history for years. Black people today continue the process of forgetting or ignoring the spirit of our history.

The process of forgetting makes decade after decade drift out of black people's collective memory. This continues today, because each generation's youth are constantly attempting to create what they view as the spirit of black people. This generational process means the ignoring of the generations that had come before them. We continue slavery's process of forgetting in this world what we helped to create. We have no remembered roots which give direction to the youth, so they explore new directions without purpose. Yesterday has no meaning to survivors! Forgetting mandates that you live only to survive. We have always survived in the hope that we, as a people, would become something greater. Should we, as a people, place any importance on our history?

Do slavery and the civil rights movement hold any importance to a band of individuals? Does the history of the African continent, in general, have any importance to a people who view the continent generally? Do we care why the process of forgetting began, and what led us to where we are today? Do we care about our history? Our roots were changed in slavery; should we reclaim them? As you can see, there are many questions we need to address, questions we cannot address until we become a people. We have achieved slavery's dream. We are just Americans, black Americans.

We must remember the one thing our ancestors fought to maintain was our oral history and culture. It was dangerous to pass it on to your children then, and it is difficult now. The collective African culture is now gone, as we have been reborn as Americans. Gone are the history and names of over eighty-five tribes! We have no idea of who we used to be. Our European/American relatives have ignored us. Our African relatives no longer know us. Most of us are not aware of our extended families here in America. We must stop forgetting long enough to find out if our people's legacy has any meaning to present day blacks.

In Brazil between 1500 and 1850, three and a half million African slaves were received. In 1835, according to Wikipedia, 51.4 percent of the people in Brazil were black. In the year 2000, only 6.2 percent identified themselves as black, although over eighty million Brazilians are descendents of those African slaves. Their new generations consider themselves white. Our new generation continues the forgetting. Our generations believe survival does not require family, education, or history. Survival only requires money. What we wear, what music we like, how we worship, what we eat, how we talk—are these actions and activities enough to define a people? We can control, somewhat, what we become as a person, but black people in America cannot move forward until it has been determined that we have become a people!

When we become knowing in this world, perceiving ourselves, we feel our existence in this reality. Our parents give us a name, and because of that, they open the book on our lives. When asked who we are, we allow others to glance at our book. Our names are the book's title. Our last names are the book's introduction. This is important in terms of family, a people, or a world view. The history of man began with an individual thought about ancestors. The phrase "my people" ultimately led to collective dreaming, the soul's belief in its ancestors, and thus history began. The recognition of the soul of the people led to a belief in a supreme being, the keeper of the old souls. As our belief in a supreme being increased, our resultant actions led to formal religions. Ancestors worship was the obvious or logical next step in man's evolution, for the ancestors were with God.

Man created the trappings of faith and wrapped them up in God, the state, and family. The support mechanisms for these three pillars became gold, precious stones, and other offerings such as food, land, and cattle. To track this wealth, which fed the state and gave honor to God, man developed writing. A writer was a profession in the ancient states of Nekhen-Nek-hen/Egypt and Sumeria. It was lorded over by the clergy. Humanity's realization of self caused all of these changes. He had a name and therefore a destiny. Man began his walk through time, building monuments we still marvel at today.

In the beginning, the ancient world was not white. Egypt, Sumeria, and Ethiopia were black civilizations. War was waged against these societies by those we would today call Europeans. Egypt and Sumeria's people were destroyed, and the victors renamed their civilization. These lands are Arab states today. The result of this external pressure was one of the reasons why African people began a movement into other parts of the continent. This phenomenon is referred to today as the Bantu migrations. As Bantu civilizations began to grow in West Africa and South Africa, they ran into European colonialism. This constant destruction led to chaos for the Bantu (Ban-tu) people. The following historical facts are presented to show how Africa went through this process of imperialism to become a continent where its people were killed, manipulated, or sold into slavery.

The destruction of black civilization in northeast Africa/Middle East and the continued defacing of black civilization in western, eastern, and southern Africa led to the belief that Africans were without souls. This racially-driven belief led first to Arab slavery in East Africa, and then to European slavery in West Africa. This racially driven belief led to Africans being referred to as a color. Thus began the final movement of those Bantu peoples, who represent all of the eighty-five plus tribes which makes up our black foundation. I believe this process began in what we call today

Egypt. Egypt was called Nekhen in 2500 B.C. It is assumed that vowels were not used in this language. They are now added, so we can speak the words. To understand, we must understand what happened in 2500 B.C., a time when nations fought over the concept of ethnic purity versus social integration, and wars were genocidal.

Africa's history is one of strong belief systems and repeated assaults on its cultural evolution. These assaults continue today, at times carried out by fellow Africans. In regard to the cultural evolution of our ancestors, the changing of our names was important to the elimination of our collective and individual histories. Racism's cohorts decided that to alter the records of the past aided in proving that no civilized human being lived in Africa, and civilization sprang from Greece. The development of Nekhen was attributed to an unknown Indo-European race, which moved south and bred with the people of the Nile valley. This gave the created white/black men the necessary intelligence to build the marvels of the Nile valley. While it is known to be wrong, this falsehood is still being printed. History is still trying to right itself because of one of its greatest lies: raced-based history. The removal or the altering of names is instrumental in the continued reverse evolution of African people.

The Egypt we know today is a view of the Nekhen civilization after its Greek and Roman periods. European scholars then colored the entire history of the area with Greek and Roman influences and images. Even when the African names are understood, geography is presented using the Arab and Greek names. In contrast, the Greek belief that this was the land of "the burnt faces" is disregarded. History was created and written to uphold some people's preconceived opinions. Supremacy was at the top of the list of those opinions, as Egypt became the land of the white/blacks in history's eyes! White/blacks is a phrase you still hear today in Africa and America.

Nekhen fought many wars to keep the white menace at bay. We know this menace to have been Indo Europeans, the forefathers of the Arab and European peoples. These conflicts against the outsiders integrating into "the children of the sun's" world often led to what is called the intermediate periods. These periods of chaos often changed society's evolutionary path. The result of these intrusions was the whitening of North Africa, and thus, the world we know today. This can still be seen today in the Sudan as the Dinka and others continue their war with the Arab north.

The pyramids are examples of why Nekhen is still known today. They wanted to be remembered, but their history was forgotten. The Arab Asians had won, so they reinvented the region's history. It was believed by the faithful that the gods of Nekhen walked into this reality by speaking their own name. This single act of creation brought nature into the realm of the living. Every part of nature's oneness was expressed by a deity, as were the various parts of the human body. This means that animals, plants, minerals, and life processes were understood and explained by the interaction of the gods. Just as the heart, lungs, and brain, work together in one biological entity, the gods of the Nile were parts of one being. That one god's spoken word belied reality. That singular god was reality. The singularity of their purpose was to be remembered. Thus, man built monuments to the various gods.

The segments of Nekhen, Egypt is history, to many lay people are often told as the actions of the gods. So when you discuss their history, remember that each god represents a distinct group of people, a province, or nome. This incident from R.B. Parkinson's book, *Voices from Ancient Egypt,* speaks of a time of descent. It addresses the creation of Nubia during the first intermediate period around the tenth and eleventh dynasties. The goddess Tefnut (Tef-nut) became angry with the god Ra. She fled to the south and created Nubia. She then went about killing men in the form of a lioness. Later, the god Thoth, in his baboon form, intervened and created peace between Ra and Tefnut. This can be retold this way: the followers of Tefnut had a problem with the followers of Ra. They did not want foreigners to live in their land; they wanted to be segregated. They broke away and formed the kingdom of Nubia. After this breakup, African influence in the Nekhen military began to wane. They were in a state of conflict, until a representative of the followers of Thoth demanded an end to this period of conflict. Nubia then became one with Nekhen again. The followers of Thoth then began killing all those who did not support the alliance. The gods of Nekhen were unified again with their African foundation, but the decline of African people had already begun.

Belief

I wish sometimes
I feel sometimes
I think sometimes
I cry sometimes
All these I do sometimes
As sometimes, I am real

Every great moment in humanity's history has been supported by a great faith; thus, history is often directed by that great faith. The understanding of religion, therefore, goes hand in hand with the understanding of great civilizations. The two faiths of the northeastern area of Africa, the Sumerian and Egyptian religions, had to be removed in order to destroy the civilizations they supported; thus, the destruction of black civilization meant the destruction of black faith. The faiths of Sumeria and Egypt were replaced with Judaism and Christianity, as the center of the world moved toward Europe. This change also continued the movement of African peoples south of the Sahara. The following statement of facts is to explain this process.

The land of the sun, the civilization of Nekhen, was always integrating large numbers of displaced persons moving south after geography-altering events, and the Saharan people moving east. This created an experiment in integration as the eastern, northern, and southern influences met in the Nile delta area. This period was the start of a series of events which would lead to the conflict over this experiment. The conflict was resolved with the joining of the sky faith of Osiris (O-si-ris) and the cult of Ra. This fragile religious agreement was to embroil Nekhen society until its demise. This generalized history was the beginning of a process which would lead to the creation of black Americans as the last movement of the Bantu.

It has always been known that the way to control man was to control his belief systems. You had to believe in somebody, to be somebody. No civilization has ever lasted a significant period without a solid belief system. Humankind spent years studying the sky, because they lived in a time of many geological events. The sky was ancient man's television. Its movements were the shows that humankind studied. This study of the sky created the Osiris/Isis myth, or sky faith. In this myth, Osiris is tricked into a coffin and murdered by his brother Seth, a story that is similar to the biblical story of Cain and Abel. His sister (the first recorded resurrection) later resurrected Osiris, and they had a son, Horus. Osiris later passed on to become the god of the underworld. The son of the new god of the underworld fights with the god Seth until he obtains revenge. This faith joined with the cult of Ra to form the religion of the Pharaohs.

There are two creation myths according to Breasted's book, *The Development of Religion and Thought in Egypt*. The gods of the Osiris/Isis myth merged with the African gods of upper Nekhen, the cult of Ra, to create the moral foundation of a civilization we know to have lasted five thousand years, according to the timeline established by Petrie. The core of the indigenous people's faith was the god Ra. These faiths had to be accepted by the people to be the foundation of the empire. Having your province as the home to some of the gods allowed the citizens of Nekhen to buy into the goals of the country. Due to religion being central to the expansion of the empire, temples and their surrounding lands produced a connection to the empire for the local populations. Each nome or province was home to a particular deity or deities. This acceptance process began with the speaking of the god's name. In this faith, a name was power.

This power produced the segregationist policies of upper Nekhen. These policies were altered to create the union that was Nekhen. This union of perceived outsiders with indigenous populations created the civilization of the Nile we now know. The altering policies were to be a source of conflict throughout Nekhen's history. The rulers of Nekhen described the outsiders as Asian. This "land of the burnt faces" attempted to limit outsider influence and blending with its people, a major point of fear for many races today. In an African country at the beginning of history, the roles were reversed, and Africans were sliding from power. History presented a new path to African civilization, one which would lead the entire continent from temples, to huts, and ultimately to slave ships.

The Egyptians claimed to be from the land of Punt, which was to have been south of present day Ethiopia. The cultural influence of Punt created Ethiopia and Nekhen. The Greeks called Ethiopia and Nekhen the home of the burnt faces. The Indo European (Asian) was the enemy. The Nekhen desire to maintain a closed society was based culturally and financially. The gold and precious stones sources were south of upper Nekhen. Other mineral wealth was in the Nekhen controlled Saudi Peninsula. The majority of Nekhen trade areas were on the African continent. Control of trade was the lifeline for blacks in northeast Africa. The results of this conflict and later blending can be seen today in the major language of northern Africa, Afro-Asiatic, and in the conflict between the north and the south in the Sudan.

One of these civil war periods manifested itself during the first intermediate period. It can be assumed that after the building of the pyramids, the union of these principal players began to unravel. The African upper Nekhen faced a threat from more integrated lower Nekhen. The outsider influence in the eastern delta was the Hyksos (Huuk-sos), or the shepherd princes, who worshiped Seth, and the newly formed Nubia, a segregationist state south of upper Nekhen. In Nekhen, this period was like the civil war in America. Three major factions were at war during the civil war period in America: the federal government, the confederacy, and the Native Americans. The north fought to preserve the union in America, as upper Nekhen fought to preserve the union in Egypt. The people of upper Nekhen also fought over the concept of integration, as did the Confederacy. The victor of this conflict was upper Nekhen, which led to a renewal of unity with lower Nekhen and created the glories of the middle kingdom period, just as the North won the Civil War and started the period of the reconstruction. Now, stay with me. You say, "Why all the history?" Well, as we began to slide from power, our journey became tougher.

The Shepherd princes created an external problem for the middle kingdom. Their influence reared its head and led the effort that forced the middle kingdom to collapse. This brought forth the next period of chaos, which was to be called the second intermediate period. Unlike American history, the fabric of the nation was always under pressure, as threat after external threat continued to weaken the segregationist foundation of the country. This external influence was the Hyksos.

The Hyksos invaders used relatives in Nekhen to gain an increased foothold in lower Egypt. Hyksos is the Nekhen word for *Shepherd Princes*. The Shepherd princes were believed to be Hebrews by some, like Osman, the author of *The Hebrew Pharaohs of Egypt*. Whatever the case, the Hyksos came to power and took the title of pharaohs and ruled most of lower Nekhen. They even extended their influence into upper Nekhen. This ended with an effort by the Hyksos to form an alliance with the kingdom of Kush. They were attempting to break the alliance, which supported upper Nekhen. This attempt failed, as the kings of upper Nekhen destroyed the Hyksos influence and forced them out of the country.

As they left, they took with them their knowledge of being Egyptian/ Nekhen. The Hyksos are thought to have slowly migrated north across the Mediterranean spreading Nekhen cultural influence. This led to Nekhen having influence on the Minoan civilization and the Greek and Roman faiths, according to Martin Bernal's book, *Black Athena*. The new kingdom pharaohs then turned their attention to wayward Kush/Nubia. While the armies eyed revenge to the south, the volcanic explosion of the period, 1500-1450 B.C. on the Isle of Thera, was to send a wave of people fleeing south, looking for a new home. This resulting mass of humanity was referred to as the sea people. They tried, on multiple occasions, to invade Nekhen.

War seemed a great substitute for confusion. The new pharaohs used conflict to insure unity. After bringing all the internal elements under their control, the Nekhen kings began their climb toward its zenith. The Hyksos underclass still existed inside Nekhen. Some believe they were the Hebrew people. Its leadership, the Hyksos pharaohs, was gone. Slavery followed for the Hyksos followers who remained. As unity returned to Nekhen, the kings turned their attention to the northern Hebrew homelands. The armies were again on the march. The suppression of segregationist African elements continued the process of creating an ever-growing, integrated country. The great pharaohs, such as Ay (Ai), Amenhotep II, Thothmosis II (Thoth-mosis), Thothmosis III, and Amenhotep III (A-men-ho-tep), brought Nekhen to be zenith during the new kingdom period. The royal family continued to change, as during this period rulers took the daughters of many conquered lands as wives and concubines. The royal family became a reflection of the general, more cosmopolitan, population.

The fall of Nekhen was due to a change in the balance of power. That change of power came about when Amenhotep III began to consider returning to the roots of the faith, a return to one God. He felt the priesthood had gained too much power. Their wealth was too great, and a return to the past was in order. The return to the concept of one God and a demoting of the many gods of the land led to political upheaval. The political root of this move was to lower the status of the priesthood and remove a lot of political competition. His son, Amenhotep IV, changed his name to Akhenaten (Akh-na-ten), and led the effort to change the religion of the nation. This led to the faith of Aten (A-ten), "the sun of god," and the temporary decline of the sun god, Amun Ra. The followers viewed it as the faith for all humankind. The Integrationist faith upset the segregationist followers of Amun Ra.

The fall of Aten and its removal form the minds of men saw a rise in the power of the old priesthood and the reappearance of the god, Amun Ra. King Tutankamen was born Tutankaten, but he was forced to change his name. Just as the followers of Aten were removed from the history of Nekhen, he had to change his name. Was this the slavery of the Jews in Egypt? According to Jordan's *Encyclopedia of Gods,* the followers of Aten (TN) later fled to the desert of the Sinai and renamed their god YHWH around 1200 B.C. YHWH was a god at the top of the mountain, a god of the volcano. This god was to be called Jehovah by 1200 A.D.

The results of this chaotic period led the nation of Egypt to a period of obsession with the priesthood as the protectors of the faith. Soon priests became kings. This led to a reduction in the strength of individual military commanders, as a methodology for the priest caste to maintain control of the country. The system was out of balance. This perceived imbalance led to the return of the children of Tefnut, the black kings of Kush. Kushite kings sent armies north "to make right what was wrong" in Nekhen according to Morkot in his book, *The Black Pharaohs*. They became the royal family of the twenty-fifth and twenty-six dynasties; they brought back the roots of the old and middle kingdoms. Nekhen was black again.

The countries of Nubia and Kush have always been a part of the equation that was Nekhen. Due to the weakness introduced by the king/priests who had come to power, Nubian armies marched to bring order to chaos and to correct the balance of power. During their reign, many temples were repaired and constructed. Many granaries were filled, as Nekhen returned to its glory. Soon future invasions would lead to its demise. As Nekhen's glory receded toward its original home, its legacy was last seen in Nubia, Kush, Axum, and Meroe (Mer-oe). As North Africa fell to the Indo-Europeans, the Africans fled to the land south of the Sahara, and Nekhen became Egypt, land of the Arabs. Racism had made its first deep mark on African civilization, as the creators of this civilization were pushed out.

The concept of racism has led to the fall of many civilizations and the demeaning of many others. Refer to the book, *The Destruction of Black Civilization*, by Chancellor Williams. Africa obviously was not spared this phenomenon, and it is still dealing with the systemic results. Racism was just an extension of man's desire to be supreme, and thus, became a motivation for war. These wars led to chaos, and from chaos came new beginnings. These chaotic beginnings led to random evolution. As societies and individuals interacted, their path became random evolution. People soon became colors. A few people write history, but it reflects the national dreams of many. The few believed that some ancient knowledge was correct and other knowledge was wrong. The few determined the color of the future.

We have seen civilization evolve on the African continent in the guise of such great states as Nekhen, Ethiopia, and Punt. These civilizations affected the development of West African civilizations of Dahomey, Mali, Songay, Ghana, and Benin. The removal and alteration of names propelled race-based history on its way. Soon the names of slaves and their people's culture would follow this road through time. Africa's evolution was on a downward spiral, moving from temples to huts, and often to slave ships.

Understanding how this historical breakdown began on the African continent, we, the children of the last phase of the Bantu migrations, must decide if this general link to northeast Africa has any relevance to our future. Do the eighty-five plus African tribes that donated their DNA to our African foundation make us an African-based people? Does our people's possession of every European bloodline make us European? Does it matter to us? Can we not see what is wrong? This decision will affect our people's future direction. An orientating belief in the past is necessary for a belief in family. Faith will give us our moral direction. Understanding the past, with a good moral direction, will show the way to the future—a future we must create, for it will not be handed to us.

Enlightenment

Who were you?
If not, no one
What did you see?
If not nothing?
What did you do?
If not, just scream
While pain covers
Only every dream.

Who were we?
If not somebody.
What did we feel?
If not pain's ring.
What did we do?
If not, just sing
While blood covers
Only everything.

What is a man?
If not a piece of God!
What does he see?
If not what he believes.

What does he feel?
If not just his pain
While tears cover
Only God's dream.

What part of our culture is African? Culture is not what you do today. It is what is passed on. Realizing that simple things are passed on from generation to generation, it is necessary to find that point of simplicity with regard to black people's future. We must find and engage a simple step that will give direction to our future and reclaim our African soul. We must create a step that does not reject rich, poor, or middle class, rather includes all religious faiths, all the various colors and ethnicities which make up, or are related to, the people who are called blacks. We must create a step that is driven by a faith in what constitutes our people and is simple enough to make the generational leap. What could that be? Are we even a people who need to discuss the future? Do our goals need to be driven by economics? Are blacks just a group of individual consumers?

God's creation is ours to finish, not anyone else's. It is what we do that decides our future. We have to stand up and change our world. Black liberation begins with minds and actions of each individual. What is the purpose of life, if not to create greatness? Is it to just pass time and cultivate a hate for white people? Is it to have children and teach them to just pass time and yell discrimination? I say, "No." It is to complete your perceived destiny for yourself, your family, and your people. Education has to be at the root of this perceived destiny.

I recall listening to a couple of healthcare professionals complain about black youth wearing their pants around their bottoms. They stated that this could have a negative impact on their skeletal structure as their generation ages. This could become a healthcare issue when their generation turns fifty years of age. The question then becomes, Whom do you speak to about the problem? The lack of a national black agenda stating the direction of our cultural evolution and a controlling council that reflects the will of the people, makes it difficult to address any problem relating to the people called blacks in America. We should have some control over what is passed on to our future generations.

Life is an evolutionary process for every person or group of people on the planet. We should begin changing ourselves, and with that change create a people with a name and a direction. Why would blacks not consider a name for themselves? Grab control of our culture and its evolution, thus creating something great, instead of just letting our future play out, as if it needs no participation from us. To create a people who will live life with pride and honor takes participation. It takes an effort by us to create a people whose souls shine above riches or poverty. We, the children of mother slavery, know we have the ability to create. As a graduate of San Jose State University (history/African studies) and a member of Omega Psi Phi Fraternity Inc., I believe that, because I was created!

I can attest that where I am does not speak to where I have been, or hopefully to where I am going. What I say is based on my life and the evolution of my love for my people. I present these thoughts merely as a conversation about all the segments that make up black America. I believe that within us lies the ability to create a people. This creation will make our hearts sing and our ancestors laugh. There are many problems with regard to blacks in America, but nothing is more important than our future as a people. We need to take the final steps in the creation of ourselves. We need to finish our creation under the umbrella of a defined people. Black people need to be a defined people with a name and a goal.

The history of the world displays the cycle of creation and destruction. All of its elements, including man, plants, and animals, are subject to this cycle. Whole species have faded into the mist of time. Man and his nation states have fallen prey to nature's cycle of creation and destruction. Man has strived to survive in larger and larger groups. Man would create new peoples, new states, new nation states, new countries, and recreate old empires. When these entities were destroyed, man would recreate them, and the process would begin again. The new entity would strive to reach its pinnacle, until it also faced destruction. This is nature's way; creation and destruction are major parts of nature's equation. Striving to achieve or to be somebody is to follow nature's law; to not try is to ignore history and its lessons of destruction.

The signposts of our interactions are best understood as emotions. We evolve as individuals and as a people. We are always wanting to achieve, and yet, not knowing how. Man is constantly attempting to learn and to understand. Yet, in hindsight, we realize change is very slow. It can sometimes appear as if nothing changes. The simple things make the generational leap. These simple things have the greatest impact on people. The greatest change is personal, as individuals begin a process of influencing all of humankind. The importance of the family as a foundation for moral guidance is necessary for humankind. If it is not there, then humankind has a problem. We often say the effort to unify is our most difficult challenge. It is because unity would affect all of our serious problems. Power and influence can be achieved based on the perceived external unity of the group. Unifying is as simple as believing. Believing sometimes is as simple as faith.

There exists within man a spirit. That spirit is our closest contact with the entity we often refer to as God. The many faiths of humanity are debated in importance, but they are the only belief systems to date that give directions to the soul. They represent the moral foundation for all of man's greatest achievements, even man's ugly achievements. A place of religious meetings often gives comfort to the human spirit. Man has needed to believe during his entire existence. Nature and the sky was man's first television, and thus, became the representations of man's first gods. To understand nature, man was shown the earth and the sky. It taught man the way to get the most out of his reality and learn the interrelationships of his reality. Our spirit has always learned from our experiences in life, hence man's moral evolution.

To believe in the soul of man, is to believe that a piece of God is in each of us. Religion has had many names, but can only have one purpose—the evolution of man's soul. The essentials of faith are the principals of spiritual evolution. Self-hate will lead to the destruction of one's people. Love of self will lead to a love of one's people. The love of one's people leads to a prideful and goal-driven life, which becomes a benefit to all humanity. The love of humanity will lead to a love of nature and a love of order. The law of natural selection offers death to species that fail to evolve, or they will be forced to change as the world changes around them. We should take steps if we want black people to move forward together. When we bring clarity to the confusion of titles and names that we claim, it will be a step in our evolution. If we believe, it will be a step in our moral evolution.

Man believes God's will and natural selection are the laws that drive the concept of growth. Black Americans, by the nature of our experience, are constantly evolving and maintain a belief in God's will. We are always looking for a new way to express our culture or our individual nature. As we go forward, we, the people, must find a new way of being black people. Webster describes black as, "a shine, a burn, the opposite of white, without light, evil, disgraceful, or dismal." Is this a name? In a consumer-based society, where money is the only god, we must not allow our progress to be limited, because we believe that power and influence are complicated issues. The concept of being black creates a degree of unity for a people from many diverse, ethnic mixes. A degree of the confusion perceived within the concept of blackness is produced by the conflict of a group, versus an individual, consumer-based society. Does the current society in which we live believe in internal group unity, or does it lean more toward the creation of individual consumers? This is a point we must decide for ourselves.

The past can only be a legacy, one that lies at the core of the soul of a people. That legacy is passed on only if you know the story. Who your ancestors were creates the plot of your story. We must take that next step in our people's rebuilding process, or surrender to being individual consumers, black, individual consumers! When a new people reject unity for the concept of being individual consumers, it has to be a learned behavior. We must accept that learned behavior, or we must redefine the face of Twenty-first Century African America through oral tradition, education, and writings. That has to be our generation's legacy to our evolving people. We must determine our direction, and hence, our next goal, for we know at the very least consumer-based societies are goal-driven. We must establish goals that make each of us a great person, and thus, pushes us toward being a great people. Our individual improvement would be our personal contribution to our people's legacy. We must look inward, and find a name which will reflect our cultural connection to the future.

Are American blacks a people? Do we exist as a distinct racial entity, or is being black merely a way to describe the results of the slavery phenomena and its resulting sexual interactions? Our blood flows from the soul of a continent with many tribes blending with all the bloodlines of Europe. Fleeing from slavery caused the joining of our DNA with the DNA of the ancient people of America. Nature and American law assisted in the creation of a new people. This new people later blended with the blood of Asia, and is still creating and changing its DNA every day. The joining of these souls from four continents, points to a human with no memory of his birth and an overwhelming desire to forget the pain, and in some ways, to forget life, which is God's greatest gift. It is life and its experiences that create man and his thoughts. It is the thoughts of the many that create a people. The essences of this life are described as God, and a child stands closest to the essence of life. Do we understand that we must remember? We must remember our roots and embrace the roots of all who have contributed to our DNA. We must remember that life has a purpose, and we, as a creation of God, must have a goal.

My life has been no different from anyone else. I have experienced and been exposed to various incidents. My emotional response aided in imprinting life onto my soul. Thus, so much of reality becomes perception. Books, newspapers, television, radio, and personal experience enhance perception. Before I was fifteen years old, I had been exposed to Baptist, Lutheran, Jehovah's witness, and colored (Christian) Methodist and African Methodist churches. I have made good decisions and bad ones, but I live with both, as they constitute my soul. In my few years in this reality, I have noticed that people strive to be different to claim an identity. Life is nothing new, but I have to tell you, it's an adventure with ebbs and flows. Our perception of ourselves changes every day, as we add experience on top of experience. As black people, we face a problem in our perception of the future. We come from many sources and backgrounds as a group of people, and unity has become a difficult problem due to our individualized perception. Thus, it makes sense that we cannot complete the process of being African Americans until we define our African nature.

What confuses us is attempting to find commonality among a people who are comprised of various degrees of European, African, Native American, and Asian DNA. This new African-based blend is the foundation of a new people. We are a people who were created during slavery and its aftermath, an aftermath that has raised us to be individual consumers, which effects our perception of unity. It is my opinion, that to establish national goals for a segment of America's population will be beneficial to the whole of the population. Goal-oriented children will create strong families.

My father's generation came from small town, rural America, and headed to the cities. My family now, as many others, serves as teachers, probation officers, firefighters, correctional officers, police officers, security guards, and sales representatives. My father, a veteran of World War II, repaired electronics for the military's Strategic Air Command. We are parts of many things, but across the board, we are black Americans. To have a name and to be part of something gives a meaning to unity. To have a name gives a face to your family. In the broader sense, it also places a face on our people, a face of our choosing, and a name to God's creation!

Perception

When I was a kid
We had a fence
Our fence, a hole it had,
And for a child
I was glad.

In the course of learning philosophy, one has thought processes when presented with a question: If a tree falls in the woods, and no one hears it, does it make a sound? For many Africans living in America, life begs another question: If a race does not have a name, does it exist? These questions speak to our perception of self. These thoughts also speak to the heart of our people. It begs for a reaction. We need to become goal-oriented—mentally, physically, and morally. Being goal-orientated leads to a higher form of personal creation. The spoken word was a source of creation in many ancient faiths. The spoken word belies our reality. The spoken word creates. When a people have a spoken name, it will create unity.

The naming of African American has been randomly evolving, and hence, we have been called many things such as colored, Negro, blacks, niggers, niggas, Negroid people,

Afro-Americans, and African Americans, and black Americans. These multiple designations demonstrate the lack of direction within the black American perception, a lack of direction that is today taking a different turn directed by the current generation. I recall overhearing a conversation between two white teenagers at a coffee shop in an upper middle-class white neighborhood. (You must understand that if I am a color, then everyone else is a color, too.) One looked at his friend during the course of a conversation and called him, "My nigga." Their friends call them white/blacks! The lack of a defined identity for blacks is driving this phenomenon. When people are identified correctly, these types of incidents will not occur.

During the long, continuing assault on African civilization (3000 B.C. to the present day) by Asians (Indo-Europeans), Hyksos (shepherd princes), sea people, Greeks, Assyrians, Romans, Arabs, Dutch, German, British, French, Italians, and Americans, many African people were assimilated by the various invaders and used against their own people. Other African people were pitted against their indigenous rivals for the benefit of the invaders. Many others were killed outright. Beginning with Nekhen and continuing through the present, the strong African empires and social organizations were attacked, destroyed, and even had their territorial names changed, so that the invader could gain control of mineral wealth and trade routes. The altering of names was a necessary process in the institution of control and manipulation.

Around 1000 A.D., an Arabic word was given to native Africans who called themselves the children of the sun. They were called Nuba, those who are worthy of being slaves. This word is a reflection of how long the assault on black Africa has been occurring. Are the Arabs referring to Nubia? It is believed that Arab slavers took over fourteen million Africans as slaves. To this day, Arabs have a word for blacks—Abd, which means slave. Arabs still raid the southern Sudan to sell African peoples into slavery in the Middle East. After years of confusion and destruction, Africans now prey on their own people, just as we, black Americans prey on our own people today. Is this a coincidence? No, it is the learned legacy of a manipulated African people. It is why we should say, "Nigga, please!"

Since slavery, African Americans have been devaluing marriage. As there are more single mothers raising children, it is understandable that the term "my baby's daddy" has replaced the term father. To continue the devaluation, calling women bitches and whores in songs and poems becomes the second step. Devaluing marriage destroys family, and the destruction of family destroys the people. In an article entitled, "Marriage is the great equalizer," Roland Warren says that between 1970 and 2001 the overall marriage rate declined 17 percent but declined 34 percent for blacks. The overall rate for out of wedlock births is 33 percent, and 70 percent for blacks. In 1950, 64 percent of black males were married. In 1998, that number had dropped to 41 percent. There is still a way to alter our direction, for God is in each of us. Bishop T.D. Jakes stated on his television show that God will bring greatness out of a great mess, but He needs our help.

The principal of separation aided in our oppression during slavery. We separated from our language, from our culture, and from our names. Our owners manipulated our allowable growth. They separated us from education. The separation of the group into controllable individuals has retarded our ability to unify during our long period of freedom. The randomness of our evolution has placed us on the wrong path. As human beings, we make mistakes and end up on the wrong path. Money and position have been perceived to be the most important concepts, as many black individuals struggle to survive. We are on the road to becoming individual consumers. We can change our path. Education is not perceived to be a primary player in this game by many black Americans. We must change that, for education and understanding are needed for all degrees of change. The individual needs money, and thus position, to survive. Were these principles merely creating red, black, brown, and yellow consumers?

We have to see ourselves as part of a larger entity, so that we will not accept the principle of separation or lose sight of the big picture. We have to find the right path. I feel that a clearer understanding of who we are would assist us, because it appears that our growth process is incomplete. This has to involve the evolution of our collective souls. The solution has to be able to influence all aspects of black America. Something has to be done. What would cause all of black America to take a single step? Some people might say that the solution cannot be simple. They argue that we are complicated, emotional beings, who need complicated solutions. No change in our direction can be simple. We need programs and funding to create a change in our society. Yet it takes a single step to begin a journey. Naming is a step that requires nothing but acceptance.

Black people's base genetic stock comes from Africa, but most of us can't trace our roots back to a specific part of Africa, and very little of our day-to-day life is African. Life has made our tribe different. We are, to the earth, a new, nameless people. We could not go home, and now our genes come from almost everywhere on the planet. We have become a universal melting pot. We must live out our destiny and play the cards that we were dealt. I was told that living life was the key to man's destiny, and that God created life. My job was to live it. Who I was would collide with life, and the resulting experiences would define my many moments on earth. It became obvious over time that first, I was defined by my name.

Experiencing feelings while living life led to my emotional definition. Emotional experiences as an individual, made me become a complicated soul. My name and my life define my contribution to my people's legacy, unfortunately only to those who experience my life's journey. Those who experience the good and bad of our people's journey perceive the life journey of our people in much the same way.

Family is the foundation of personal history. If you followed your genetic ancestry back to the beginning of slavery in the United States, you would be directly related to 16,384 people according to Shriver and Kittles in their article on genetic ancestry. If our evolution had been normal, there would be approximately 1,221 major family groups, which would compose African America's population (twenty million). Our color gives us a people, who represent the final phase of the movement of the Bantu people, a movement called the Bantu migrations. The migrations are the final phase of the movement of Africa's children. Our nearest geographic kin are the people of the Caribbean, who got off the boat before we did. Our Native American cousins, and our European forebears, complete the genetic foundation. We were hauled to America as slaves. Since then, we are still changing. We are moving forward without looking back. We need to look back. We have just opened our eyes, and we know we are a closely related people. The majority of our history is before us. We are a new people from an old stock, and as a child, most of us wondered what part of our evolution we were we to witness!

What makes our history? Most of us are taught that it is events and trends over the course of the human experience. From the plains of East Africa to the cities of America, we nameless souls, like all of humanity, are constantly in a search for God's purpose, a reason for living. I say again, God, in his many forms, is man's moral direction. Beginning with individuals, to groups, to cities and states, man's future has always been tied to degrees of unity and faith. All the major faiths have various beliefs as to God's affect, on man's history. Unity is also a base of faith. One thing is for sure, man has a lot to say and do with his history, and unfortunately,

God only helps those who help themselves. The naming of groups of people led to the creation of clans, and ultimately the creation of states and nations. Using war and trade as the roadmap, and faith as the compass, man began his walk through time. We nameless people walk, too, shrouded in the mist.

I always wanted to experience life from a position of growth and to become the best person I could. I found that change is only hindered by a person's belief in its existence. When you do not believe, change will not occur, unless it is forced on you. Change was forced on us, as a people, by slavers with a desire for gold, and a society with a desire to control and intensify their wealth. As a result, Einstein's theory of an equal and opposite reaction created a new people. We are a people who would have surprised the creators by still existing, a people created by American institutions and laws. If you have Negro blood, then you're Negro, was the concept that determined who belonged to this new race, a people created over hundreds of years and many DNA mixes, a people created in slavery. `

Slavery and its aftermath produced overflows, those who wished to escape the burden of color. The inhabitants of these gray areas were not sure where they belonged in this color-based society. Some tried to assimilate into white society. Many did not want to belong to a people who were yet to be named, and yet, many did. We were confused. We learned power and control from the slavers. We also copied the concept of classifying the coloreds into moral arenas of good and bad. Let us learn from our social history, and use power and control to change one individual at a time. It is never too late to create!

Let us take the concept of the house nigger. It is fairly understood that house nigger and Uncle Tom are seen as insults, even to a person in the Twenty-first Century. I see the existence of this insult as a measure of where we have been and how much social progress we have made. The mere fact that the insult still exists is a statement that we are on the wrong path. As we make positive steps, should not negative steps begin to be less apparent? We should mark our progress based on the removal of negatives. That should be seen as a strong measure of growth. Living the good life based on honor and respect is as essential as fighting the good fight to the future of black America. The quality of an individual's actions is multiplied to reflect the actions of a people. We are all responsible for who, and what, we create.

The removal of the concept of field nigger versus house nigger has to be seen as a road sign of progress. The use of incomplete names empowered the house nigger versus field nigger concept. Incomplete names and degrading names were part of the core of our racial driven slave existence. A name similar to the master would give you greater power. This would also separate you from your people. This would take away from the soul of the people. Names aided in the evolution of status in the slave community. It also has to aid in our evolution in this our country.

Self-determination has to be a core concept, of change. It can be simplified by saying we cannot yell at anyone, until we yell at ourselves. Naming ourselves could begin a process that would turn our self-image around and redirect our future. An adopted child searches for some knowledge of his biological parents with a name as the goal of that search. As our self-image improves, so will our condition, not by money, but by effort. The reclamation of some parts of our past will help us see the future. A name speaks to knowledge of self. It can also help us speak to reclamation of the past.

My name started my life. I am an individual member of a family, as dysfunctional as it may be. My life is an example of the confusing struggle that my people, black people, face in America. Each individual member of the family represents a part of black America. Each individual member of the family actions contributes to the outsider's perception of black America. Our mark is left according to how we affect the souls of others. Therefore, it can be deduced that genes and perceptions are constantly creating and recreating black America. Once you realize we have the power to create, that power has to be treated with respect. I've found through DNA processed by African Ancestry and family stories, after years of wondering, I am Tikar, from the Cameroons; German, the colonial power in the Cameroons; and Cherokee on my father's side; Temne, from Sierra Leone; Jamaican, and an unknown Native American people on my mother's side.

Realizing I have African, European, Native American, and Caribbean roots broadens my perception of being black. I have also been perceived as a militant, soldier, student, police officer, dishwasher, skycap, farm worker, assembly line worker, car washer, and a parking attendant. Do all of these characteristics define me as an individual black consumer? As the genetic child of slavery, I have been experiencing life with a degree of confusion. I was designated by a color, and yet, I still believed all people were the same in my child's view of the world. Everyone was red, black, yellow, white, and brown.

Yes, I remember when I was a child; I felt everyone's life was similar to mine. I believed we all lived in similar areas, and we all had hand-me-down shoes. I was wrong, as my thoughts turned out to be just the dreams of a child. Our goals are based on dreams. Contentment is found in the heart and delivered via action. Yet, we are always struggling to accomplish greater dreams. Imagination creates even greater dreams. My dreams forced me to begin puzzling out the mysteries of life. I wondered "why" about too many things. Why do we live? Why had we been created? What was I to do with my life? As I began my search for knowledge in the early fifties, the rear fence was my first obstacle. The world inside my head screamed to be let out of the box. However, all of life has limitations. One summer, that freedom came, and we were out of the yard and on the trucks at 5:00 A.M. My brothers and I went to work in the fields, picking tomatoes.

Evolution

The bullets flew
One night in hell
As red lights flipped
With clanging bell
The radio cracked
Numerical sounds
As in the beginning,
A man was down.

The ominous sounds
Of a shotgun round
Blended with pistol fire
As banging doors
Scared the whores,
Who scrambled cursing to the ground,
As the radio blared a code thirty-three,
goddamn, a man was down.

Reality places a stain on childhood, as you begin to define yourself in the eyes of your peers. So what is an African American? Is it a person who comes from the union of an African and an American? Is it a person with some

African blood, or is it just a dark-skinned person? Is it a person who is a descendent of relationships with the slave master? Is it just descendent of slaves? Is it a person who marries one of the above or their children? This lack of definition leads to internal and external mental conflicts for black people. As souls, we are defined by our actions, and thus, we become individuals. This occurs just because we believe in it! What we look like, what we wear, and how we talk, defines us. How does that apply to our people? How are they defined, or how should they be defined within this reality? Each black individual's life and ethnicity is slightly different, so where is our common ground? We need to find that common ground as individuals and as a people. We black people are always looking for some commonality, but often we place the individual at the root of our random evolution. We must learn from experiences of our ancestors. We must change.

My mother always believed in cleanliness. She felt that being clean was related to class. She was right. Personal health lies at the root of greatness, for health is necessary to grow old and become wise. The root of this thought process could be in the cleaning of wealthier peoples' homes, something many members of my father's generation did. Yes, she was right, cleanliness is next to godliness. This simple thought process led me to assume that I could make myself into what I wanted to be by merely placing myself in various controlled situations, which would create certain mindsets I wanted to achieve, thereby growing by each experience and having some idea of what I would end up being. Circumstance had been an important aspect of our creation. My thought process excluded negative influences on my growth. In the end, the concept of fate blindsided me. It did not allow me to see the future. We, as a people, cannot see the future, so we relied on God's will. I had always been taught that the future was God's to know! When I was the co-chairman of the Revolutionary Action Committee of the

Black Student Union at Sacramento City College in 1967, I was reacting for the benefit of the future, a future I could not see. I was to be surprised at where it led.

My father told me that in order to change something, you had to do it from the inside. Who you were would have an impact on the world. You could not do it by yelling from the sidewalk or by acts of violence. My father was a member of the NAACP. As a shy introvert who first found his voice and his expression of anger with the nationalism of the sixties, I could not understand why, as a people, we were treated the way we were. Why did we have to get angry to be heard? What was I to do? Follow the turn the other cheek peace movement, the rising African Nationalist movement, or the aggressive Black Panther party? Therefore, I did my yelling as co chair of the Black Student Union's Revolutionary Action Committee. This action group later divided into Black Nationalist and Black Panther party camps. Most of my associates became the core of the Sacramento branch of the Black Panther party. I fell prey to the Draft Board in 1969, after a brief takeover of the school administration building. I recall a military representative telling me, "We don't care about your student deferment." I was learning, and life was teaching, so away I went to join what I later found to be an entirely separate society.

After my indoctrination into this culture, basic and advanced training, I served and learned in the U. S. Army military police. This new culture shed a light on the one I had departed. I found that coming from a large family, and my pledge period with Omega Psi Phi Fraternity Inc., really prepared me for my adventure into military life. I was back to believing I had to survive and still want to grow. I began to realize life wasn't what I had assumed. Life had become a series of roles, and we were all performers. The army gave me the skills of a confinement specialist in the military police, an ironic state of events, as role-playing blended with life. I felt God (a power greater than me) was teaching me something, so I further sank myself into another experience, this time seeing it through my nationalistic eyes.

The U.S. Army, in a 300-man military stockade at Fort Campbell, Kentucky, extended my first lesson in social manipulation. The stockade presented a lesson that changed how I viewed the world around me. One day while taking a shift in segregation, I had a conversation with a prisoner named Sweeny. Sweeny was member of the 101st Airborne Division. He was telling me how he related to his neighborhood and to his military unit. I began to reconsider the concept that identity had a lot to do with the creation of, and/or the destruction of, a group or unit. He showed me that your actions become your legacy. During the conversation, someone called my name. The next thing I knew, Sweeny was holding a razor blade, molded into the handle of a toothbrush, to my throat. The force of the "Jimmie Gillette" made me angry, but forty-five minutes later, when I was no longer a hostage, the incident was finished. We completed the conversation while he was in the hole. Youth and a view toward survival in the compound ultimately overcame my anger. It opened my eyes and allowed learning from another source—negative incidents—as some things are never as they seem.

That incident drove me to research unity-based identity. I found answers in the history of the creation of the first recognized all black military unit, the Fifty-fourth Massachusetts. The unit gave identity to its members and a legacy which is still intact. Units in the American military draw pride from their names. I began to read another book on black military history. Many of the black military heroes impressed me by the honor they displayed, both in combat and out. They fought for an identity. They were warriors. I realized honor was a necessary component for a group that had to function within another society. Without honor, the group would become a deadly cancer cell.

Violence created us, and a fear of violence continued our oppression. Violence has been a part of our history; it has been a part of man's history. Black entrepreneurial slave owners, as did the KKK, took advantage of this fear of violence to create fear-driven markets, which took advantage of black people. They were the first black pimps. Years later, we continue the process, as we create more fear and death in our own community than our perceived oppressor. To fix this, we need to participate in law enforcement, the military, hospitals, and the fire departments throughout this country. This is necessary to stop negative players from having a greater impact on our community, and to begin to see the end of black on black crime. We need to do this, because we need to show a greater love for self, family, and our people!

A cancer cell will destroy rather than complement the body. An example of this would be an out of control military institution. An out of control military could destroy a society and/or its direction. One rogue cell could destroy the human body. One white blood cell can aid in saving the body. Law enforcement and the military are necessary to ensure the protection of the neighborhood, the life of the body. White blood cells fight the enemies of our body, just as police officers and soldiers are supposed to fight the enemies of our society. In the same sense, white blood cells are apolitical; their only function is to enforce survival within genetic perimeters. In a perfect society, our military and police should perform the same!

Sometimes violence enforces the rule of law. When it is, it is best done by individuals, who act and function in the society like white blood cells in the body. They carry out their function, but they leave their personal opinions at home. It is still a dream in our communities, but there are those who are trying. I was taught as a compound supervisor in the U.S. Army to use fear of violence to control the stockade's population and the base actions of the incarcerated. Living through this experience meant learning to handle various human reactions to adverse circumstances. I concluded this meant that honor and respect had to be a key component of any evolution within this reality. Inside the compound, knowing oneself was important, so one wouldn't become a victim of this system of fear we administered. We also needed to resist the effects of confinement on free people. Once fear infects the soul, it creates a cancer. Medication was often used to control fear and rage in the jailers and the detainees, and yet, suicides happened all the time. Fear has to be controlled and understood, as cancer cells have to be controlled within the body.

I left the service with the rank of sergeant specializing in confinement, and returned to school and my second family, the brothers of Omega Psi Phi Fraternity, Inc. I returned to school with an evolved perspective on what it meant to be a member of a culture within a culture with over three hundred years of fear-induced social manipulation. I finished my degree in history/African studies at San Jose State University after taking some time off to improve my financial picture on the assembly line at Ford Motor Company. At Ford Motor Company, we were forced to stay on the property, for the exit gates were locked. We were always under surveillance by management. The line never stopped unless there was a malfunction, which we, the workers, loved. We worked fifty-eight hours a week for the money. I left Ford with my understanding of slavery again enhanced in regard to the effects of pseudo confinement on free men and women.

The effect was the same, as if we were confinement personnel. That realization sparked a need for change in me. I needed to continue the evolution of my spirit. It appeared to me that as a people, we were not making any progress, and neither was I. Social revolution for a segment of the people was not the answer. Something simple had to be found that would create a personal revolution, a simple change that would inspire great change. A simple change in my life was also in order. In 1977, while my father was fighting cancer, I took his advice, and that of those nagging cobwebs in my pocket, and joined the San Jose Police Department in California.

In 1978, after my father's passing, I began preparing for another period of training. I believed in constant individual growth as a way to be all you could be. I realized some people acted as cancer cells and brought only pain and suffering to my world. Man has always strived for honor in an effort to be godlike. Striving is worthwhile; the journey produces growth. Many men only strive to make money and get next to a woman. If the scope of their struggle is narrowed to sex and money, then honor has to play a larger role. One needs honor, tradition, and acceptance in order to exist within another society and morality, so as not to destroy oneself. If the society kept you on the outside, your people might become dangerous to that society, as the barbarians became dangerous to Rome.

Life's journey led me to a new place. There I was, twenty-nine and a probationer in the law enforcement world, which still called black people Negroes, striving to grow as a black man. I was now with those whom I had always viewed as the enemy. It did not take them long to prove to me that my thoughts were not without merit. I was interviewing a prisoner, when a group of detectives gathered outside of the interview room. They began to say how niggers were not about nothing. They knew I was in the room. The prisoner I was booking was under the influence of PCP, a mind-altering drug. He looked at me and said, "See, you're still a nigger." I learned that even this issue could not be addressed. I was told that being thin skinned would not assist me in keeping this job. So much for progress, as the cancer cells were inside the police department as well! Survival overrides many emotions, a most interesting set of circumstances, which my ancestors knew well.

Ten years later, while driving southbound through Louisiana, I was pulled over by a state trooper. The trooper walked up to my car, and asked, "Where you goin, boy?"

I replied, "That way, sir," and showed him my police I.D. He stared at me and asked for the badge. I showed him my badge, and he walked away without saying a word. There I was in 1988, and what had changed? I was the first black permanently assigned to the narcotics unit, and the first black assigned to the intelligence unit of SJPD, a progressive California police department. Was I an instrument of change, or was it all about the money, position, or just need?

I felt we were a tribe so lacking in direction that we could only follow the dollar bill, even if it meant killing ourselves, and there I was, chasing the dollar bill for survival. I met some brothers in the police department who were more interested in personal growth and money. Some black officers could not see the big picture. Some black officers understood our position and our people's plight. We had many perspectives. Our direction was still survival, as nationalism was not our responsibility. As we chased the dollar bill like the rest of our people, life wasn't getting any better. The National Black Police Officer Association and the National Organization of Black Law Enforcement Executives worked for our people. They were, and are, instrumental in the fight to integrate blacks into the police world.

We were fighting for our existence in the American police world and losing sight of the fact that we were our people's representatives. Specific needs divided us from the mainstream. We were warriors without direction, but we were warriors! This is what we had become, in my view. As individuals, we joined the police department and were taught that we were all "blue." They wanted me to be blue, not another color! There is a reason for that train of thought; we were to be individual consumers.

Sometimes you just have to hold on and experience life, for the ride is in progress, whether you want to go or not.

Progress sometimes can only be made by adding your small part. That progress could kick start our personal revolution. Life never takes you where you think its going. I then waited to see where my survival in blue would lead me, knowing nothing stays the same, but a love of self will lead to something greater. Change leads to creation.

Changes

I often walk
However, not often see
In search of the unknown
My understanding goes out
But always returns
Just me!

Being a Negro slave was once our identity. Beginning with resisting the slave trade, many of our people died fighting to control our future. Our leaders stepped up, from Nat Turner to Martin Luther King, and still progress was slow. Our last effort to take a step forward was controlled and altered by the deaths of Malcolm X and Martin Luther King, and the actions of state governments and the FBI. As we look forward, our people are still a work in progress. We feel a bond with all of our people, regardless of their real color, bloodlines, or wealth. This bond sometimes only displays itself as a nod of the head, as if knowing there is an unfinished destiny. Young blacks do not acknowledge this bond, as something is missing from their soul. Long ago, it was defined under the 3/5 law that if you have Negro blood, then you are a Negro. The 3/5 law was once a principal that aided in the creation of our people.

Slavery was the birth process of our people—a very long process. The slave owners turned us into a color. We were not African. We were a color. That is when this began. We coloreds had no civilizations. We were beasts of burden. We, Negro slaves, were not capable of creative thoughts. This is because no civilization was ever built by us, because we were just created. When we were freed to find our own way, we continued to be Negroes and coloreds. We had accepted the masters' labels, because we knew no others. Action was taken against us as a group, not as individuals. Rules and laws were passed and enforced against us as a group, not as individuals. Somehow, we bought into the concept that we were a group of individuals with no links to each other. Unity will create power, and individualism will remove power. If its existence is questioned, that power doesn't exist. Thus, belief becomes fundamental and thinking a necessary component of that belief.

This group of individuals has stayed a color for reasons that can only be tied to the impact of slavery. This group struggles with pride, honor, and respect. This group has rejected unity as a first step towards power because slavery had reduced survival to an individual process. Survival was not even a family process, because slavery had such a major impact on the family unity. Even today, we still have problems. I was watching a reality series called "Being Bobby Brown," and was amused as the Brown family was keeping it real! I wanted to ask the question, Where does honor, pride, and respect lie while they were keeping it real? I felt I was watching a perfect example of random, interactive evolution controlled by children and lasting decades, a perfect example of why we need to increase the priority placed on pride, honor, and respect. These additions would cause the reality show to make a glowing statement instead of what we saw!

The legacy of the concept of individual survival is black on black crime. The Junior Black Mafia vs. everybody, Crips versus Bloods, and El Rukans versus Black Gangster Disciples, this cancer lives amid deteriorating schools and neighborhoods. This cancer is fed by a constantly evolving drug problem. Is living in the ghetto the goal we wanted to achieve? A desire for money was first adopted as a goal because we needed to survive, but as years go by this individuality-driven goal begins to feed off the group. A cancer of this type cannot help but to assist in the killing of the collective group. We have a drug problem, whose distribution is controlled by other people, yet we fight for the right to profit off our own death. We are merely the victims, but we are the ones whom law enforcement targets, because we have turned on ourselves repeatedly during incidents of violent crimes. Some of us became wealthy and developed degrees of power, while most of us merely gave way to the youth. The people who control the distribution are often not targeted as we created the headlines, and thus, the squeaky wheel gets the grease. First heroin and then cocaine, ravaged our communities, as we ravaged ourselves. Heroin, cocaine, and rock cocaine are still with us. As we learned to survive one evil, another would rear its ugly head. All of this was meant to be another method to hold us down (God's will?), or are we holding ourselves back?

Who is holding us back? Why are they trying to hold us back? Who is trying to stop us from making that first step called unity? These questions almost sound like generational paranoia. Unity comes from within. The system's reaction to unity is out of date because it exists as a throwback to slavery. We react to the remnants of this old system, because our reality was created in slavery and it's aftermath. We now engage in enslaving ourselves after years of a systemic reaction. Anyone could have seen this coming because some blacks even owned slaves in an effort to copy those in power! We saw power and desired to be the oppressor. We are our past, so slavery lies at the root of all of African America's problems, and hence, reparation rests at the center of our forward movement, for only a people can receive reparations. We need to change the game because anything can be changed. Reparation will aid in ending the obsession with our painful birth. It will aid the healing, as this nameless people exit the mist and accept our birthright.

African America, its many religions, multiple colors, and mostly poor people, needs unity and a collective dream. Unity will aid in our evolution and the dream to add honor to the way of our people. Where do we go from here? Every faith teaches us to follow the ways of a spiritual soul. To be godlike is the way of a soul being directed toward a collective dream. It is the path of the faithful of every faith. To be godlike is the path which leads to the greater good. It is individual in its path, and inclusive in its conclusion. It is the way of human beings; it is the way of natural selection. It is the next face of black America, the face of those who only want to be all they can be.

Who are we going to be? Do we want to be individuals and be recognized for self-expression? Do we want to be a people with a goal and a purpose, where honor and respect are more important than making money? Are we going to have a goal, or stay where we are now, a people who were born in slavery? We are a people who are in an ongoing fight for financial acceptance from the slave owner's descendents. I use the term financial acceptance because money is the root of this system. It is necessary for us to unify, if we choose to step into the future.

Our goals have to be generated by our minds and carried out by our souls. We can be what we want to be, we only have to believe, believe and gain knowledge through education. Is it possible that we will have to take a step backwards in time in order to take a step into the future? We might have to look back to slavery and to all the unremembered who stood up and were killed. We might have to look back to all those who stood up, by reading, and died. We must remember the millions, who were merely thrown into the sea or died during the middle passage, and the thousands who died in combat proving our worth as warriors. We must feel for the fathers and mothers, who maintained our families in the face of adversity, and the Negro intellectuals, who forced mankind to accept that we were thinking individuals years after they began pretending we were not. We must remember the thousands who died just for reading the Bible. We must respect and honor those who have come before us by living our lives with honor and respect. We must undertake a path which leads to the future. We might have to revisit our history to have that collective dream again, for history is the foundation of unity. Only without a developed mind can you not have history.

The Bible says in the beginning, God created man in his own image. Current knowledge says man began his journey in southeast Africa. According to some, man did not reside in Africa. No man lived in Africa, only the beast, a beast that would work for you and would respond to a pronoun. This is what was believed by the participants of the slave trade, both Arab and European, and those intellectual and business parties who benefited from racism. Many believed God had not come to Africa, that the population had no soul. Without a soul, you were not real people according to the faiths of the day. We must put this slavery thing to bed and protect the soul of the people. We must realize it was our birth process, and our future is in our hands. Instead of feeling shame, we should be proud of how we survived as a people through such a painful birth process, and we know slavery was painful.

We are not the first people to be born in slavery. We are the first with the various mixes of African, European, Asian, and Native American DNA, which make up black America. We should be proud of all the great souls who have brought us to this stage of our development. Inventers, athletes, soldiers, sailors, scientists, and teachers have pushed us into the future. We have overcome obstacles like slavery, the KKK, and segregation. We now face heroin, tobacco, cocaine, alcohol, HIV, and disintegrating families, and yet, we have reached this period in time as a people. We must protect the future and remember the past. We must project, the real soul of our people, a projection based on our love for our people. We must change.

Humanity is still learning, and a lot of that process is random. Physical and mental interaction with other persons and groups, without direction, will recreate a random group. That group will become a victim of random evolution. It will affect all around it, randomly interacting with other groups and creating a random result. If you allow these random events to be the bases of your social evolution, you can only call it God's will. This process causes man to move from permanent civilization to transient people and back again, as nature and the war for control of wealth kept man's development in flux. The movement of African people, written about by Dr. Greenberg, could symbolize this process. He was a linguist, who studied the spread of people over the African continent. The Bantu people are the major African language group. Their movement across the African continent is called the Bantu migrations. Was this movement the result of the growing desert in North Africa and/or the military assaults of Indo Europeans in the north and the east, or both?

The Bantu people have been spreading south across the African continent for thousands of years. Due to desire and circumstances being determined by man, the Bantu people have been creating and recreating themselves for years. This is why there are so many language groups in Africa. In Africa during the migrations, as a group became too large for survival, it would divide, and the new entity would name itself. Sometimes war, nature, or just plain survival would spur this event. The slave trade was the last major influence on the Bantu migration. This led to Bantu and other sub-Saharan communities blending with others in the Arab world, South America, the Caribbean, and North America. Although influenced by degrees of integration, these are the final migrations. The last chapter of the Bantu migrations is still being written. We, as a people, need to control our destiny and begin to write the last chapter.

Random interactive evolution is seen from our perspective as God's will. From our perspective, we cannot perceive its intent. It has no perceived direction. This is because, to the faithful, God does not explain his master plan to humanity, but only helps those who help themselves. If this was God's way, then slavery in North America has to be looked at as a birth process with religious implications. Our creation was God's will. Accordingly, God has spent hundreds of years creating us through desire and circumstance. It is as if we were to be created without knowing what purpose we would play in the overall plan. Therefore, we are a nameless people, who have yet to make the next step, as if our future is a secret we must conceal. Many people believe life is predestined and directed by God. That disregards man's ability to influence his life's direction, a belief that removes man's responsibility for his bad decisions. We are the result of God's will, but our future will be determined by the direction of our free will.

Why do we do it? Why do we except this reality? I believe it is because we do not feel capable of creating change. We must step out of the darkness into a lifestyle that reflects honor and respect. We must walk with fear, and with its guidance, live life. We are nameless Africans living in America. Due to the determination of slavers, Negro became our classification. We accepted the created slave culture and passed it on to our children. We accepted the classification of Negro. We accepted money as power and its pursuit as the goal of one's life. Money determined who and what you were in our society. We followed the only path we could see. We attempted to follow, without guidance, white America. Some of us even became slave owners! How ironic, even we could become oppressors. We began to push for position and influence, as a methodology for achieving freedom. "Money talks and bullshit walks" became a catch phrase for a few generations.

The child, who was left outside of the mainstream, began to use non-mainstream methods to survive and evolve, and thus, began our second slavery. Crime was seen as a way to create and achieve power. Criminal activity against your neighbors was accepted. Black on black crime has grown and has never decreased. It has taken over from the KKK as our greatest terror. The death of our youth by another for disrespect is the ultimate "dis," as we now struggle with our own civil war, brothers and sisters killing brothers and sisters, black people terrorizing our own, retarding our own, oppressing our own growth out of envy. When will it end? When we stop it!

From many directions, we continued our struggle for the inclusion of our culture, as a method to see our spirit grow. During a period of enlightenment, we changed our classification from black in Spanish (Negroes) to black in English. Thus, we became "blacks." It was a major step. It was important, because it was an effort by all of us to take a step together. It did not happen quickly, but soon we were on the same path. Black Americans are still attempting to try to control our culture and determine who we are. Now, what we are is very diverse persons who come in all shades, and yet, are all called black and African Americans. We are a nameless tribe of Bantu peoples, searching and constantly growing. The Bantu migration has ended in the Americas, thanks again to the Europeans and Africa's original slavers, the Arabic people.

We have forgotten ourselves, and now change almost daily. God's creation needs a collective dream! We now worship many faiths: non-denominational Christian, Baptist,

Methodist, Catholic, Islamic, Jehovah's Witness, Buddhism, Mormon, and other faiths. We have married and blended with many races, and yet, are all black, a nameless tribe living in America, even though none of us are truly black in pigmentation. We now belong to the second largest groups of Africans living outside of Africa in the world today. We only speak our owner's tongue and have no knowledge of our lineages. We black Americans have a name that is yet to be spoken. Nevertheless, alas, we do not know who we are, for our birth process was too long, and we have almost no knowledge of self.

The oral tradition was used to keep the past, when writing was not in use. Slavery destroyed our tradition of oral history, and left us as unknowing representatives of the last phase of the Bantu migrations. We are the children of an experiment in social manipulation. We cannot speak our own name, so we refer to ourselves as a color! Our identity had been beaten from our souls. Our history was wiped from our minds, and education is necessary for recreation. Thus, we see the rest of the world as various colors, a bad concept to teach a child, but not a bad one to teach a nigga! We are unknowing, and we accept whatever rests on fate's plate. We do not need to determine who we are—we know it. We just need to say it and pass it on. It is sad that fads drive our culture more often then God's will. We are blind to the importance of the process.

The Christian parable once used by the church to refuse aid to God's children, says that God only helps those who help themselves. We can only help ourselves by becoming more and more educated. Part of the problem is that the school system will not teach what is necessary for black Americans to make such drastic changes and build on them. History begins with "civilization's creation in Greece." What this means is that we are taught Western history, or the story of the white man from his perspective. This is one of the methods used to alter our history. We are taught that we are individuals, and we will achieve only when we obtain money. We act as if it is over, and we have become what God had intended.

Our history is the history of the African continent and North American continent, the old and the new of this world. Direction has to be given by the soul of the people, and not Park Avenue advertisers, music videos, and sports icons. They are a poor replacement for fate, and an even poorer replacement for collective dreaming. We are a growing child, and life is about living and growing every day. It is our responsibility to learn and pass on the history and culture of our people. One day, we will become what God intended. That path has to begin with a name. We should begin the walk. I recall sitting with a very good friend of mine, discussing the state of blacks in world history. He felt that man's soap opera has played itself out repeatedly. He felt that we were not special, considering the totality of man's past, man's journey. I felt that we needed to view ourselves as special, special enough to give our people a name.

Our history began, as did all of humanity's, in Africa. What has happened to Africa helps us to understand where we are today, and why we face the obstacles we face in today's world. The effort to control wealth by destroying African civilization is an ongoing process. Turning this process around by building a people has fallen on Africans in the Twenty-first Century. To understand the building process is to understand man's place in nature's equation. Africa's history is one of survival. We must have a clear direction to deal with the many socio-economic and health problems facing Africans in the world today. We must struggle to gain control, or our culture will continue to mutate without our direction, taking us to a future not of our choosing.

Remembrance

Claiming many parts of humanity,
We used to be, the lost
Nameless souls of slavery, hiding.
Who claims the dispossessed's thoughts?
Obsessed with only life's jewelry
Sometimes we, remember, who was bought
Confused consumers, becoming…
Where are my Levis and my thoughts?

In general, we black people come from so many different African tribes, that our only view of Africa represents the continent. We view its history in total, even if we cannot determine how we are related to that history. This is a curious set of circumstances for a nameless people, who are the result of an intercontinental event. Our view of the world is thus unique, when compared to any of the world's people. We, therefore, need to remember as much as we can. We need to go back in history to understand race based history. It was race-based history which created the events, that created black Americans. We need to understand the flow of history, so we might understand ourselves. Race based history was the justification for efforts to control trade, and thus wealth.

It was often necessary to create chaos and war to justify changing history. Controlling trade routes translated into power

We African Americans have had many periods of random, interactive evolution. We also must learn and recover from these periods of chaos, if our history is to continue. America's last civil war was the civil unrest associated with the civil rights movement. Reunification, for nations and people, generally follows periods of chaos. These are efforts to reestablish normalcy. That has not been accomplished in America yet.

Earthquakes, volcanic eruptions, and droughts, caused some periods of instability, and pestilence affected group growth. The desire to control trade routes and the sources of the gold and minerals were the reasons behind the constant conflict in northeastern Africa. The invasions of the Hyksos (the shepherd princes), the sea people, and the Assyrians were examples of other people's efforts to control trade routes.

Punt and Ethiopia were the cradle of civilization, not the Tigris River valley. From these civilizations came Nekhen, Sumeria, Kush, Nubia, Meroe (Mer-oe), and Auxm (Aux-m). Nation building continued on the African continent in the face of Eurasian, and later Arab, efforts to control that part of the world. Was this the beginning of the Bantu migrations, or did that begin with the first intermediate period? Regardless, it began around this period. The spread of people from this area's civilizations found their way to west and south Africa.

The kings of the new kingdom were said to have had a residence in the West African city of Gao. This civilization, which was similar to Nekhen, was Dahomey. Over a thousand years after Nekhen's demise, the Nekhen tribal system reappeared in West Africa. Nekhen and Dahomey (Da-ho-mey) both believed in a dual cosmology, living and dead, east and west, royal and common. They both employed professional soldiers, and the defeat of an enemy met subservience and tribute under both systems. The Temne people of Sierra Leone wore helmet masks during ceremonies to resemble Nekhen animal head gods, and they believed in magic. The Yourba of Nigeria believes that their people were descendents of an Egyptian. The Yourba civilization was part of the process that led to Mali, Ghana, Songay, and many other great West African states, as the Bantu people continued their spread south across the continent. The Zulu of South Africa also claimed to be descendents of Nekhen kings. Nekhen knowledge was spread with this movement of people. An example of this transference of methodology is the existence of Nekhen reed boat knowledge in the Sudan and in Mexico.

The spread of people south out of the Nile Valley was caused by wave after wave of invaders attempting to live or control the Nile Valley. These were efforts to control the trade routes to sub-Saharan Africa, and thus, the sources of gold and other minerals. Nekhen's control of these routes was the source of its rise and the reason for the Eurasian push into northeast Africa, and, of course, Nekhen's ultimate decline. The major mineral and gold mines lie south of Nekhen. The West African civilizations developed in a response to an external effort to control the sources of trade. In addition, it was the reason for the downfall of many civilizations in West Africa. When the mineral sources dried up, slaves soon replaced gold as the new trade item. While new names and cultures were continuing to appear (Afro Asiatic speakers dominated North Africa), the Bantu speakers spread south to the cape, ultimately pushing the Khoi-San speakers into the Kalahari (Ka-la-ha-ri) Desert. The Bantu migrations were moving into a new phase, one that was influenced by greed, as blood proved to be as precious as gold.

The last great upheaval in Southern Africa was the Mfecane (M-fe-ca-ne). This event began when a Zulu impi (regiment) was sent to collect tribute. Disobeying orders, they took everything the people possessed. This made the tribe of people homeless. This dispossessed mass took from other people to survive. Soon they joined with the now homeless Zulu impi. As the mass grew, the entire region's, social structure was pushed into chaos. The Mfecane destroyed the social fabric of the entire area. Therefore, when the Boars trekked into the interior, they reached an area that was not populated. They assumed no one lived on the land. This was the impact of the Mfecane. The impact of the Mfecane spread north into the lands of the Shona (Sho-na) people of present day Zimbabwe. The impact was the arrival of a new people, a people who had split off from the wandering mass of millions created by the Mfecane. These new people were the Ndebele (N-de-bel-e), or Matabele. Some say they were the Zulu impi, and their new women, which started the social upheaval known as the Mfecane. When the Ndebele met the local Shona, relations broke down. The resulting conflict between the Shona and the Ndebele still affects the area today. It can be concluded that rejected social groups often renamed themselves as a way to begin again.

An example of naming is the Temne people of Sierra Leone. They were created as an army from the empire of Mali, which was dying. They met and blended with a segment of the Baga people. The general of this army, Farma Tami, is considered the founder of the Temne people. Another army of Mandinka (Man-dinka), under Mansa Kama during the fall of the Songay empire, added their cultural evolution to the Temne people. Therefore, nameless people naming themselves were an African process, which was necessary during a time of displacement. The Bantu people continued to spread to other parts of the world on ships, slave ships. After the move, no cultures were created; no tribal structures were put in place. This new slave institution had new rules.

This was a holocaust for Africa, with millions dead during the middle passage. From this fire came a new entity—nameless Africans. The Asian of Nekhen times blended with African people and became the Afro-Asiatic speakers of our day. They became the Arabs of our time. The continued conflict between Arab and African is still evidenced in the Sudan. This genocidal conflict is a continuing symptom of the destructive movement against Africa, which has been ongoing for forty-five hundred years—so long that today, African people worldwide now inflict their own pain, some say, as a systemic response. The systemic response is a learned response displayed by African people around the world.

As we realize that our needs produce our goals, our wants become material desires, and money becomes important. Black-on-black crime creates the neglected future we face. The story of the Tikar dynasties in the grasslands of the Cameroons is an example of black-on-black violence. With the decline of their influence, their enemies preyed on them, selling their best into slavery. From a tribe of over a million souls, they now number three hundred thousand. We must step out of the darkness, and take a step toward the evolution of our souls by understanding our history and determining where we want it to go from here.

Greatness for an individual has, as its foundation, a name. The concept of naming a person, place, or thing can be considered by some to be insignificant, but to many it is very important. When an Arab man had a child with an African woman, that child would become an Arab child. When a European man had a child with an African woman, that child became a Negro. In both cases, the changing of your cultural name obscures your past identity. During American slavery, we were only given first names. Our last names were the last names of the owner, if it was even spoken. If we were sold, we were given the last names of our new owners. In time, as the individual slaves walked through this nameless maize, everything began to break down.

As generations passed during slavery, we lost our names, history, and culture. They gave us the narcotic of stupidity. We could not read, and we could not think. They treated us as dogs. We fought this process through slave revolts, and many of our ancestors met their death. It seems the only way to fix things is to reverse this process, define our group, and obtain a name. We just need to declare ourselves, for names reflect the groups past, present, and future. That means, since the search for our history and culture has begun, we must search for a name. All of these actions will lead us down the road toward greatness.

Nameless people have always fought for the right to be somebody. As Americans began to see themselves differently from the English, they renamed themselves. The history of the American Revolution is the story of a search for a cultural icon and name recognition. Negroes, slave and free, fought in that war, and the War of 1812. After these conflicts, those warriors were returned to slavery. Our only goal was to be Americans, but they would not let us into the house. Over 400 slave revolts on ships, and over 250 slave revolts in America, symbolized by Denmark Vesey and Nat Turner's revolts, show we always fought to be free. Therefore, if humanity's history is about the search for identity, then why was it such a big deal when African slaves addressed the concepts? Our unity is at the root of white fear, even to this day. The slave revolt, which created Haiti, has been used as an example for why black unity had to be resisted. Naming oneself is not just an American or an African phenomenon, but a human one. Naming one's people proceeds unity. Maybe in our case, naming one's people can create unity!

Could it be that the process of naming ourselves would mean we would not be Americans? I believe that identity means strength. Why are we not like other Americans, with names that symbolize us? If we become a stronger people, then our country would be stronger. The resistance is not based on any apparent logic, but on a desire to retard the growth of this child produced in slavery, and to keep him outside of the house. A child raised outside of the family, like a pet, will not grow normally. Unable to sit with the family and be recognized as a member, his or her cultural growth will result in chaos and random, interactive evolution. If we are allowing individuals to determine personal preference in regard to culture, or to allow another method to bring forth that culture by happenstance, is, in fact, cultural retardation.

Throughout our history, every effort to progress was met with anger. Slave revolts were met with anger. Reading was met with anger. New black settlements were met with anger. Blacks in the military were met with anger. Marcus Garvey's Back to Africa campaign was met with anger. Education was met with anger. Malcolm X was met with anger. Martin Luther King and civil rights were met with anger. The Black Panthers were met with anger. School integration was met with anger. Everything, except for chaos, is met with anger. Thus, anything which offered a direction or a purpose was attacked, and unguided growth was allowed to lead the way. Stupidity was to be the way for black people. We were nameless and took the classifications we were given without any thought, as if nature had meant for it to be this way. Unguided growth was seen as the will of God, and thus, we accepted random, interactive evolution and chaos.

To say we are Americans, niggers, African Americans, black Americans, colored, Negroes, Afro-Americans, blacks, or niggas is merely a representation of the chaos that comes from not having a name, or the goal of obtaining one. The confusion is only deepened when you observe the growth period of our people. Criminal organizations grew as fast as education in most of our communities. It is believed that the institution of slavery taught violence to our people.

Violence was seen as the representation of power and success. Confused people with no collective dream of their own existence are going to be doomed to slow growth and periods of failure. As failure was accepted, crime grew, and the constant recreation of our people continued. Our growth continued without collective dreams. Collective dreams are the roots of family. Collective dreaming is the foundation of culture. If there is no we, the greater we will not exist. The soul of the people would not exist. Being without the soul of the people, blacks kill blacks in greater numbers. Therefore, who we are has to be defined. Clarity begins to occur when you view slavery in America as the birth process of a new people, not an example of power, a birth with a very long period of labor.

Organizations built on small groups have at their foundation the goal of taking a number of individuals and making them think and act as one. Shared suffering, shared songs, shared knowledge, shared experiences, and the goal of membership forms a band of brothers. This process was refined for the institution of slavery to include forced membership, if you care to imagine taking people from over a hundred language groups (tribes) and blending them together over many generations, forcibly removing their knowledge of self, and then banning their language and their religions. Then, adding contact through sex and circumstances, with people from many European and Native American bloodlines, what would you have—a new people, or a nameless nigger? I believe you have a new people, a people who have forgotten their bloodlines and their cultures. We are a people who were created in suffering, a people whose thoughts and beliefs are still evolving, because they were forgotten, and whose only goal is, and was, to survive.

This newborn baby would have to have a name, claim its heritage, and declare its language, in order to have accomplished the goal of survival. This accomplishment would have added membership into America's band of brothers, but we were kept outside of the mainstream, nameless with only a goal of survival. Had this been done to a child, nameless and raised outside struggling to survive, what would the impact be? Would he or she grow to be a teacher, or a lawyer? Would this person fight for the people who kept them outside? Would they be a negative influence on the society? Now, add naturally occurring, genetic interactions over one hundred and fifty years, and here we are, still nameless and slightly aware of our birth process, still fighting for acceptance and trying to survive. This emotional period in our development leads to fights and misunderstandings, but learning aids in getting through that growth process. The lessons we are taught, and the dreams we create, become the foundation of future experiences.

What do you call this new child—just American, African American, black American, Negroes, blacks, or niggas? Slavery removed names, persons, places, and things in order to remove collective dreams. These dreams were replaced with the masters' thoughts, actions, and responses. We have fought our way back, but we still need to reclaim our collective dreams. Whatever you call it, we are a child just recently removed from the birth process. No one speaks of our ancestors because we do not know who they were, or when they lived.

Our history is evolving. Each generation paints a different picture, and history hangs the painting, but the big questions remain: Who are we? and Where are we going? As children grow and learns to apply goals to their dreams, they become adults and live their lives, never knowing their impact. As a tribe of people, we have yet to gain control of that process. Naming will begin the process of gaining that control. We have names as individuals, but the process is incomplete. Losing one's self in the American dream is all right, but it is not, and has not, been the way of others in this quilt called America. We must decide, as a people, if our history has any relevance. If we are a people, are we just dark-skinned citizens of the United States of America?

Creation

The child stares at me
In addition, I retreat
My world was lying, at my feet
Fear was tugging at my belt
From a world I had not felt
I cried and slid
Into my quiet space

The fear remained with me
It invaded this space
My world underneath
Where we would meet
My fear tugging at my feet
He placed the world at my fingertips
We are one, flowed from my lips

The dust I kept away, sometimes
As I fought wars on cotton mountains
The floor I kept waxed
As I lived life on the dusty slates
Fear created thoughts in
As we left knowing,
Our place was to create

Is it the name that creates a culture, or is it the people who believe in that culture? Throughout African history, the movement of people has led to the naming and the classification of new tribes. These language groups would, in time, define their religion and their political methodology. This would lock in many other aspects of everyday life, and they would become a people with a developing history and an evolving culture. They would become what we call a tribe. I know I am taking a complex issue and really simplifying it, but we are discussing the growth of a newborn. This birth is straightforward; simple people carried it out. We are the descendants of those who were brought here, but we were created here. The slave owners were not intellectuals, but they were the instruments of our birth. As human beings, we make things complicated in order to restrict access, and thus, create power for those who understand the creation. We were created and made to forget the creation. If we choose thoughtful growth over random, interactive evolution (chaos), then we would take toddler steps toward naming our people. Interactive growth is random and haphazard, and by its very nature, it can destroy and create without a moral foundation.

Faith-based civilization began in Africa. We should be proud of this fact, and place faith at the foundation of our people. The African societies of Nubian, Ethiopian, and Punts were fundamental to the growth of the Nekhen civilization, and hence, the faith of Ra. This religious system was the foundation for faith-based civilization on the African continent. It brought order and purpose to its people, much in the same way the ten commandments of Christianity and the eightfold path of the Buddhist faith gives direction to individuals and their communities. Man's belief in God and the spirit representatives, Jesus, Buddha, and Muhammad, represented and directed man's moral position. It was necessary for growth. It was also necessary for control, regardless of whom you believe.

On the African continent, the religion of Ra interacted with the Sumerian faith and the Hindu gods of the Indian sub-continent. The Bible says that Abraham of the Sumerian city of Ur taught the Hebrew people. The Sumerians were called the "black head people" and claimed lineage to the people of Ethiopia. They were victims of genocide around 1750 B.C. Their religious knowledge was passed on to the Hebrews, and hence, it played a primary part in the creation of Judaism. The Semite Akkadian (A-ka-dian) victors took their cities and raised their own empire of Babylon in the Tigris/Euphrates River valley.

The gods of Greece and Rome found their roots on the African continent in Nekhen, and many were just renamed Nekhen gods, as was discussed in Martin Bernal's book, *Black Athena*. The Jewish people became a people in Nekhen. Their religion also evolved in Nekhen. Some believe that the faith of the king, Akhenaten, was another great influence on the evolution of Christianity. Akhenaten believed in the sun of god. During forty years in the desert, the worshipers of the sun of god, the followers of Akhenaton's religion, began to change. As this faith changed, Yahweh (Ya-way) was born. Therefore, the Christian faith was jumpstarted in Sumeria, and kicked in the pants in Nekhen. This faith was taken and given direction by the Roman emperor Constantine. This biblical conference established the Bible as well as, the conflict between Christianity and Islam that we see today. All that came before it influenced Christianity and Islam, and both evolved out of northeast Africa.

The principles of all these faiths give direction to man's greater goal. These principles give directions on handling interpersonal relationships, and give support to the proper way to function within a society. Faith has been a needed commodity throughout humanity's history, for it brings direction. For four thousand years, the religion of Ra in Nekhen/Egypt maintained that society and was the driving force behind the wonders they produced. African America, the child whose birth has been analyzed and written about so many times, often walks without direction, and is still obsessed with the pain of its birth. The nameless people still struggle with their past and their future, but religion has been one constant. We believe in multiple religious faiths. We needed faith to overcome the obstacles that had been placed in front of us. Faith in God has taught us how to live with death and to accept what we perceive as God's will.

Black folks believed obtaining land, money, and other means to survive would be all that was necessary, with our belief in God, to obtain the American dream. We were wrong, as Jim Crow laws, the KKK, a refusal to educate, and the rejection from mainstream America brought it all to an end. Segregation and hate led the way, until Martin Luther King and Malcolm X participated in the process, which has slowly led us away from the brink. We attempted to gain power in the neighborhoods, with the family as the core of the belief system. We tried to limit heroin and other drugs in our communities. Yet, repeatedly, drugs always seem to find their way to our neighborhoods. The resulting damage to family and community aided in taking us back to the brink, on many occasions, as heroin, cocaine, and then rock cocaine pushed us to the cliff. We need to control our neighborhood and ourselves.

The reason drugs slowed African America's growth was that it destroyed families and made us the target of law enforcement. Large numbers of black people were placed behind bars, and many families were destroyed. The suppliers were not targeted as vigorously as the users, for the drugs were coming from overseas. We were also targeted because we were the source of white America's fear. In the fifties, what drove the police agenda? Was it the fear of drugs being sold by blacks and flowing out of the bad neighborhoods and influencing the good neighborhoods a police agenda? In this period, it was believed we needed controlling because of the fear that we would make too much money and alter the economic order. This fear, that we would make too much money, caused black dealers to be targeted by the law enforcement organizations of the day. This phenomenon has hampered blacks since the 1920s.

I remember being in the judge's chambers in 1987, while two cases were being settled: one white defendant from a wealthy part of town, who had been caught with two ounces of powder cocaine, the other was a black man with five small rocks of cocaine. The black received three years in the state prison, and the white received six months in a drug rehabilitation program. This disparity in justice had been going on for generations in America. Too many of our efforts now lead to unfulfilled dreams. Thus, we have evolved into a society which distrusts whites, their society, and their police.

A wise man once said that we start as simple beings and become emotionally complicated souls. We make ourselves act out roles, not caring what the role's impact will be. We create pimps, whores, cops, drug addicts, lawyers, and correctional officers. Many individuals become bus drivers, cooks, waiters, and teachers. Some strive to be ball players, doctors' nurses, and health care professionals, while others become soldiers, sailors, clergy, thugs, and politicians. These professions are the roots of our reality. They create, as well as provide, a future for individuals, as our realities lead us to death. Can you not see what is wrong? This creation of reality should be controlled for the benefit of the individuals participating, and their groups' image.

A group of slaves evolved into and created a reality that they were allowed to play in. They ultimately began to fit into this reality's boxes, and the boxes negative worlds. Their limited exposure to the system limited their ability to grow outside of the box. The confusion increased the stress of not knowing the system. They only knew that money was necessary for survival. Unity was not necessary, nor were large, extended families, which needed money to survive. The key to surviving as a people in this reality is throwing out what boxes your people belong in, if they are exposed to a legal way to obtain money. All of the people have to have a legal way to obtain money. In black America, most have few methods to obtain legal money.

Any organization that creates unity creates power, but without unity, individual consumers are created. The units of power are in the shape of pyramids, allowing only a few to stand at the top. The world is full of these pyramidal structures, and a small number of people know the keys to the top. Often, it requires a change in personality to participate. Individual consumers lay at the base of the pyramid. Our connections to individualism are what confuse our efforts to come together.

The creation of a tribe, or a named entity, would not be counter productive or anti-American. We must first understand that we are a tribe, one created by God in slavery, segregation, and through years of persecution. The numbers presented by the Shriver/Kittles article on genetic ancestry paints a picture of 1,221 major family groups. This hints at the close relationship between African Americans, as by now all of these families have intermarried. The primary language of this new tribe is English. Many people speak it, so we would have to be a tribe instead of a language group. The rejection of culture is an un-American principle. The Samoan people have a chief, and they respect their elders. They might fight each other, but in the end, they are still family. They are a tribe of people who in today's world always reflects a pride in self and in their people. No people who have come to these shores have been forced to give up their culture except us. We have a right and a duty to reclaim and rename our people, and to do it with purpose, honor, and direction.

This nameless tribe's participation in the wars of our country began to be seen as a method to bring us forward and into the house. Units like the Fifty-fourth Massachusetts, Twenty-fourth and Twenty-fifth Infantry, and Ninth and Tenth Calvary, set the stage for the growth of our warriors. World War I led to a renaissance in black America. World War II and Korea further defined the freedom we all craved, and led to the civil rights movement. Vietnam, Grenada, the Gulf War, and now the war on terror, have brought this nameless tribe to the world's military present. We are still fighting. In a time when combat is based on the precept of devotion to your brothers in arms, we are as willing to die as they are. In combat, we have proved our worth and our understanding of freedom's sacrifices. The problem is that no matter how many died, the contributions were downplayed. A warrior and his leaders must live their lives with honor, and sometimes die forgotten by the many.

There are those who would ask, What is the purpose of naming a people who already have a name? Well, Negro is Spanish for black; black still addresses color, and colored is obvious. African American is a general designation, which lacks the specifics you would find in Africa as exampled by the Kikuyu (Ki-ku-yu), Maasi (Maa-si), Temne (Tem-ne), Ibo (I-bo), Ashanti (A-shan-ti), Yourba (Your-ba), and many others. In America, where you have English, Italian, French, German, Spanish, Irish, Mexican, and many other designations. Therefore, in order to bring our people into the future without the socially binding concept of color, we should name ourselves. Our children need not see the world as red, brown, yellow, and white people. They should see the world for what it is—identity based and nationalistic systems. We do not belong to these systems. We, a people, who come from the oldest genetic stock on earth, should belong. The melting pot we represent should be represented in the identity based nationalistic systems.

Some African visitors to this country have described us as black-white men because we struggle so hard to have what he has. We are Africans, who speak English and live in

America, but a people of African stock nonetheless. We need to give honor to our ancestors and to give praise to God for his creation, or decide to be only individual Americans. This nameless tribe has to have honor. Its people have to live with respect. As some adopted children need to find their biological parents, we need to reclaim our metaphysical soul. As we look back, we know our ancestors are dead. We know the first thing that was taken from them was their name, the name of their people and their people's culture. In Africa, slavery was not abnormal, but your culture and identity were not taken from you.

If the first thing taken from us was our name, then that should be the first thing we reclaim! Why should we not reclaim, by creation, our name? In our case, we already have a culture. We created it first. We just need to control its evolution. It can be like the proverb, "my kingdom for a horse." For want of a shoe, the horse was lost. For want of a name, our people might be lost.

The acceptance of slavery as a birth process will also begin the healing. God put a lot into our creation and at some time, we will understand why. A people who took a meticulous God three hundred and fifty years to create should not be left without a title to their book. I would think God would see us as remiss, if we failed to give a name to his people. We are beginning to stand up as new people on the world's stage. We should have a name.

So how do we do it? One method can be a regional essay contest. The winners of this go onto a national ballot, voted on by all black Americans. Why should we do it? Criminal organizations, by enticing our youth, are taking the lead in the search for the collective dream. Should we let them? We have to embrace all of our people—the poor, the needy, the rich, and the famous in our collective dreaming, so we can all go forward together. In a country where the individual is more important than the group, a name is the easiest way to embrace all of the people.

A criminal organization often derives its strength from its name. Oak Park Bloods, 69 Ville, 5 Deuce Gangsters, the El Rukans, and he Black Gangster Disciples are examples of names that create power, dress, speech, and a history for their members. They also attract the children to dreams of being powerful. Names give power to its members. Names like the Mafia, the Tong, and the Yakuza, speak volumes. The thug life offers an alternative to living life with honor and respect. The thug life is the result of random, interactive evolution. It has led to Mexicans killing each other, depending on what part of the State of California they live in. It has led to blacks killing themselves over colors. If we allow this to continue, God only knows where it will lead. We must love ourselves enough to make good decisions, for our public actions define who we are. We must always think of our people when we make decisions that will affect the future.

Our decisions create various forms of the future. Street gangs, prison gangs, and their associates have had a defining effect on the societies they have met via random, interactive evolution. The dress of the youth of today has its roots in street and prison gang dress. Music videos, hip hop culture, and gang life drive a generation's efforts to transform language. Music videos have created an acceptance of nudity, and hence, strip clubs are on the rise. They are causing a change in the relationship between black men and women. Black men are now always referring to the pimp game. The developmental process of this nameless people has been altered again.

Interactive evolution is actions and reactions without guidance or purpose. Unity means accepting everyone, but pimps, whores, and gangsters cannot be the leading creative element. Faith in a system of honor and respect should direct our belief in self. Random, interactive evolution, or just letting it happen, is not worthy of a people striving for greatness. Love of self is greater. A young man comes to mind who was so intelligent that high school was not stimulating enough for him. He was a writer of short stories and poems, and he was an up-and-coming rapper. His understanding of political events was way ahead of his peers. His first love was rap. He felt that in order to be a respected rapper, he had to live and experience the streets. He even felt that jail was a maturation process. This is the impact we have on our children. This twelve-year-old was lost in the gang life. These are the children we need to save.

An organization draws strength from its name, and mimics techniques in order to compete. The name that was taken from us has yet to be replaced. The story of the rise of the Zulu nation is one that shows the power of identity. The name of the Ama Zulu came to be the force behind the rise of the nation. Their warriors' ways made the Zulu name feared. In the end, they created a power which rivaled the Spartans of Greece, and with military innovations that rivaled Napoleon's France.

Creating a tribe, or entity is and was, a powerful endeavor. We have everything in place to make the next step in our evolution. We merely need to do it. The Zulu people, at the height of their military power, possessed an organizational structure that was similar to street gangs in our inner cities. The original gangsters were like the inner-circle of advisors. The shot callers were indumas (in-du-mas) (leaders of impis or regiments). The memberships were the warriors/gang bangers. Lastly, there were the women and children. Both organizations used the fear of death. The use of death brought interdiction from the neighboring powers. In the case of the Zulu, it was the British Army, but in the case of L.A. basin gangs, it was local law enforcement. The major difference is that street gangs evolve as a sub-culture. This tribal sub-culture swept inner-city America and spread its influence to suburban and urban America. They lacked honor and respect as part of their foundation and became a cancer cell.

These gangs needed to have a moral position in order to be a positive influence to the greater society. They lack honor and respect. This dooms the sub group by turning it into a social cancer. During Hurricane Katrina, this social cancer was reported on television. They reported gangsters and thugs raping and shooting at rescue vehicles. Using just hearsay, the media painted us as thugs and animals to the world. When reported that it was not true, there was no effort to repair our image. The media said, "Oh, well," and moved on. As black Americans, we also found it was easy to believe the media coverage. In hindsight, we have to see that our souls are not complete. We need to control our own image. We need to name ourselves. As the Last Poets stated, "Niggas are scared of revolution," because we are afraid to take the easy step toward our rebirth.

Becoming

Slave faces immersed in bling
Forgetting honor for hoodies and things
Flashing colored faces, feeling good
Leaning toward Park Avenue and praising the hood,
Slipping away from the future
running on videos, chains and hip hop

Grabbers sliding in baggy jeans
Wrapped by a desire to sex what they perceive,
Steal it; take it for it is your things
Gold inserts cover decaying bling
As crotch-grabbing mindsets are,
Taking us down to consumer dreams

The fated journey of a man through life, or a people through time, has as its foundation social unity. In an effort to move forward, a lack of social unity can lead to disaster. I recall an incident on a mountain in California. A major storm was beginning to drop snow on Mt. Whitney. Fear of an approaching storm was driving backpackers off the mountain. A group of three people were giving up and starting to drop their equipment, while still high up on the

14,500-plus foot mountain. Two experienced packers, friends of mine, told them to keep their equipment and to follow them down the mountain. They felt unity would assist everyone. The new unit soon decided on the best way to survive, and then separated during the walk down. This division soon led to death of two of the group. These deaths were because of a lack of unity and trust within the group. A lack of unity and direction will doom any effort to advance or survive. It will overpower intellect and common sense.

If we are already a people, then is our only classification American? We were born here, and our roots are in the southern states. If slavery did not create us, then are we merely black, individual consumers, a combination of a majority of the races that comprise the United States of America? In this case, any unity or race-based conversations would be unnecessary, as we would be only Americans. That would be an exceptional state of affairs. What do we want to become? To become a people within a people, you have to have unity, honor, trust, and respect as fundamental principles! Staying an individual would mean we are only Americans. We would be the first people in this country to take that position. The creation of the trappings of a tribal culture that lives in Twenty-first Century America would benefit the country and us. It would answer the question of whom to pay reparations, the people, for we represent our ancestors. Let there be no doubt about that.

There have been many jokes about reparations, but as Randall Robinson detailed in his book, *The Debt*, the reasons for them are numerous. We need reparation to rebuild families, increase small business participation, and assist with education. The only real benefit would aid families, as they were the first to be destroyed and are still being degraded. That is why reparations should arrive in the form of tax breaks for wage earners, the allowance of deductions of college expenses for African American families, and 1 percent small business and home loans.

Did the use of free labor have anything to do with the development of America as a country? Did this free labor allow the colonial plantation economies, which the new nation relied on, to develop into a world market economy, i.e., tobacco and cotton? Fighting of the civil was for cheap labor. The northern industrialists wanted blacks to come north and work in the factories, while the South wanted to maintain its agricultural labor base. The moral issues surrounding slavery were insignificant to this fact. The president of the United States promised reparations, although that promise might have led to his death. He knew that forty acres and a mule would guarantee the rightful integration of slaves into American society. The killing of President Lincoln occurred because the South did not want to share its wealth with freed slaves (40 acres and a mule). That bullet cancelled a debt. Today, we must approach this process differently.

The simple step of naming our tribe would have a huge impact on our future and the world. *Tribe* is a word I will use to express the soul of the people. It merely means that we exist. We are home. It would mean we are not a color, and neither are the other races. It would mean, as it is true with other people, that we must keep our motherland in our hearts and in the foreign policy of this country. Our perception of ourselves would be different, so maybe the internal color conflict represented by the "high yellow versus the darker the berry, the sweeter the juice" statement would end. Maybe our perception of the colors black, white, brown, and yellow, as presented by the followers of racism, would disappear with a greater understanding of our own identity. I hope that the phrase "Uncle Tom" is banished to the history books. The removals of negatives in our evolution are signs that point to the future. To be great, we must act great.

We must create, as our ancestors have done before us. A person's worth is nothing without honor, a warrior is nothing without respect, and a person is nothing without a soul. The peoples' soul has to be preserved. All that is missing is a name. We need a name that will secure the soul of the people. Our relationships are in place. Our religious institutions are in place. Freedom has nurtured our relationships to Africa, South America, and the Caribbean through random, interactive evolution. We must further define their direction. We need to establish relationships directed by our leadership. Our leaders need to be accountable to our people and entity, not to various sources of money they may receive, regardless of whose money it is! The fear that our leaders will be killed means we should have a tribal council, which gives direction and interfaces with our government for the protection of our civil rights. As our unity becomes greater, America will become greater. An America with a greater black influence will render a greater assistance to the motherland, and negative statements by Japanese prime ministers and Mexican presidents will be part of our forgotten past, along with the phrase "Uncle Tom."

Due to the fears of some in white America, much in regard to race relations hasn't changed. I still think that development of our warrior class has to continue. The movement into these professions has always meant a greater acceptance into American society. Our warriors need to have a code of honor. Our warriors need to be respectful, as we build families, neighborhoods, and the future. Our warriors are not "Uncle Toms," they are heroes and should not be replaced by gang bangers in the eyes of our community. We cannot fight the system, so it is necessary to join it, and transform it with a lifestyle of honor and respect toward all of humanity. The transformation of the legal system must occur because it oppresses us. Police see poor people as the criminals because poor people created their fear and wanted their property. Now, we oppress ourselves.

Our warriors should be, and are, men and women who live with honor and respect. Black soldiers, sailors, police, and firefighters are some of the current warriors of our tribe, as are many more that the system has destroyed. As a police officer, I responded to a neighborhood disturbance in 2003. After being there for a while, one party called dispatch and asked for another officer. She demanded a replacement because I was black. My sergeant refused to send another officer, and he told me to leave the call. Some people refuse to change, and their fears are blinding. Some still believe minorities cannot police them. They can only follow their instructions.

We need to participate to make sure that what occurs on the street is correct and applied equally. It will not change law enforcement overnight because man cannot change overnight, but it will change the system ultimately, and it will change us as a people. It is never too late to create. Our identity will be established, when a name is given to us. We will have more reason to exert influence on American policy, domestic and foreign. We will be a key to America's future in the world because we have always been important to American social evolution.

My growth as a black man is secondary to our growth as a people, but they go hand in hand, for I reflect our people. I have vivid memories of two meetings; one occurred in 1971, and the other around 1985. During both meetings, the black component of the 553d M.P. Company of the U.S. Army and San Jose Police were addressed separately about perceived internal racial problems. In both cases, there was an inability by the organizations' leadership to understand the spectrum of black opinions. The spectrum of opinions was greater in the police department than it was in the military, in 1971. To narrow the spectra of opinions, is to do our people a disservice. In both cases, we were individuals, but they painted us as a group. In the end, they were looking for individual weakness, so they could alter the direction the group had taken. Due to lack of unity and inability to control the direction of our people, the divide and conquer tactic is effective. This most important tactic will not die, as long as we are individuals.

The dream has to continue. I am, and we are, a work in progress. As my evolution is continuing, so must yours and our people's. I have a name, and you have a name, so must our people have a name. This naming we must do for ourselves. It is just a small step. All that has happened has led us to this time in history. The time is now. A people marks its place in history by its use of opportunity. It is, therefore, our choice to be either individual consumers or members of a proud people.

We are the greatest symbol of America's melting pot. Sex and circumstance have driven God's will. We have to accept our current reality, but we can alter our future. We are African, Native American, European, and Asian. This, of course, creates huge family groups. It is also why we must view what we create from the larger sense. We are a tribe of people who are very closely related. No other group represents these bloodlines. Our blood represents the earth. We, without prejudice based on color or hue, can begin the development of a social system that would be to the benefit of the country, the world, and ourselves. We must acknowledge our links to this earth and bring greatness out of a great mess.

Life, in its basic form, displays the importance of the concept of unity. In real life survival is a core concept. The following story again reflects how emotional conflict will alter life's goals, and make it difficult to survive. A group of us were backpacking in a northern California mountain range and using llamas as pack animals for the first time. A discussion about carrying more weight caused a group member to become angry and walk off with his llama and two dogs. He lacked faith in the decisions of the group. His anger blurred his vision, and he became disoriented. He soon walked by our destination. Shortly afterward, he was lost at 8,000 feet in a northern California wilderness. He tied his animals up hours later and started to climb a high spot to attempt to locate us, but it was too late; he had gone too far.

We had stopped hours before at our discussed destination. We were packing in bear country, and he was lucky to have a dog with him. Unable to locate us, he soon found he could not locate the llama and his other dog. Unable to locate them, he wandered in the wilderness for thirty-six hours with no supplies. The next evening, shortly before sundown, he had walked into another camp. He was bruised and bloody, but in fair shape. Afterward he was asked about the incident, and he stated that after he relaxed he began to think clearly again and found his way back. These are the lessons you learn through experience. A little anger and disunity can produce hours of fear. Unity and clear thinking create power, and that power leads to clarity of purpose.

In Washington, D.C., during the million man march, clarity of purpose shone brightly. The march was a gathering of men in an effort to reclaim the collective dreams of our people. If you were there, or saw it on television, then you know what I mean. Even though a march without women might be interpreted as anti-family, sometimes brave steps must be taken, and sometimes the warriors of the tribe need to redefine their direction. Did it happen? Did the million man march impact the collective dreaming of a people, of a child? Yes, it did! It is not clear, but the dream is out there, and we were watching that morning on the mall. That morning my friend, Vic, and I walked onto the mall in Washington D.C., it was an awakening experience for both of us. We met lawyers, doctors, farmers, firefighters, truck drivers, and cops. We met students, homeless people, thugs, and hustlers. It was a great day! Later that day, a homeless brother from Virginia was collecting money to place in the containers along the mall. He had an armful of cash. He placed the money in the container and checked his clothes for any other bills he may have missed as we stood by watching. To us, it was a special moment, one small step. I saw and felt our dream! The future is created by man's footsteps. This future will include us, if we want to be there. We can only look forward. We already are a people. We just do not have a name. We must reclaim some of our people's traditions, reach back, and reclaim some aspects of our African nature. We must scream for reparation, as we screamed while they beat our names and our history out of our memory. The blood of our ancestors demands it. The unknown members of the 1,221 major family groups demand it. The memory of the children who died on the street, demand that education become a top priority. The warrior is a wise and respectful soul, not a thug. He has to have respect, honor, and above all, knowledge. We must act as a people, for with clarity of purpose comes peace of mind. We must define the chaos, and move forward with the evolution of our soul. Words create thoughts, and actions create the future. For as a great poet once stated, we must be "the masters of our fate and the captains of our soul."

Lastly, if we choose to be individual black consumers, then I would suggest our black men and women join police departments, fire departments, probation departments, confinement agencies, and all the wings of the military in greater numbers, just as black men looking for equality joined the Fifty-fourth Massachusetts, Twenty-fourth and Twenty-fifth Infantries, and the Ninth and Tenth Cavalries. I say this to the many of my nameless brothers and sisters who reject the "white man's system." You need to get on board if we are not going to be a unified people. The primary reason is, as individual consumers we need to be financially secure, we need a benefit package to secure the health of our children, and we need retirement packages to secure the future of our elderly.

These are not the only jobs where this security can be achieved, but we must join these organizations as a means of changing the economic status of so many of our poor families. The only business on the street is trouble, and the only retirement plan is prison or homelessness. This will not happen if first we reap the benefits of the educational system. Then, we must attempt to dominate the professions that bring services to our neighborhoods and to our country, for with participation comes power. The threat to individual life is no greater in these professions, than it is in life itself. Individuals should not refuse to work for their people or their country.

To refuse to belong, is to ultimately accept a homeless death. Thus, black people are faced with a decision. We must join the educational process wholeheartedly, and thus the professions of this country in greater numbers, or we must join a new tribe of Africans who place their people above money and position—where honor and purpose have meaning, or perhaps we can do both. We need to go where we can, and prosper wherever we go. I say we do both!

We must make life better and enjoy it, for it is one of our gifts to the future. My life in law enforcement showed me the many results of poor decisions. It showed me repeatedly that the small decisions we make often have a major impact on our lives. It also taught me how crime influences various family groups' social evolution. My path was not the best or the only way, but it was my search for knowledge. The world is going to be what it is going to be, but we need to believe we can change ourselves. As a people, if we do not adopt goals we will eventually fall prey to the lessons of history, and soon we will only be a footnote in time. I do not believe anyone will remember a consumer. Your contributions to our legacy will stand higher as a member of a group of people, than as an individual or a consumer. When we make ourselves better, we make this country great; it has always been that way. A people whose goals include a life of honor and respect will add to the legacy of themselves and America, and then our future is ours to imagine. If we do not create, our random paths will create without direction, and as they yelled,

"Back in the day…"
Turnkey knock it down
It's time to take my meds
Pop a pill or maybe nine
I've got to go to bed.

Knock it down, you silly clown
This place is messing with my head
I'm locked up, and my girl is gone
And I can't even go to bed!

Sources of Knowledge

Gailey, Harry	*The History of Africa* Vol. 1 & 2
Breasted, James	*The Development of Religion and Thought in Ancient Egypt*
Parkinson, R.B.	*Voices from Ancient Egypt*
Bernal, Martin	*Black Athena*, Vol. 1 & 2
Clark and Engelbach	*Ancient Egyptian Construction and Architecture*
Aldred, Cyril	*Akhenaten, King of Egypt*
Diop, Cheikh	*Civilization or Barbarism*
Redford, Donald	*Egypt, Canaan, Israel in Ancient Times*
Oliver, Roland	*The Dawn of African History*
Gardiner, Alan	*Egypt of the Pharaohs*
O'Conner and Kline	*Amenhotep the Third*
Ryan and Pittman	*Noah's Flood*
Stiendorff and Steel	*When Egypt Ruled the East*
Robinson, Randall	*The Debt*
Clayton, Peter	*The Chronicles of the Pharaohs*
Stringer and McKie	*African Exodus*
Clark, Rosemary	*The Sacred Tradition in Ancient Egypt*
Tudge, Colin	*The Time Before History*
Watterson, Barbara	*The Gods of Ancient Egypt*
Morkot, Robert	*The African Origin of Judaism*
Franklin, John	*From Slavery to Freedom*
Diop, Cheikh	*The African Origin of Civilization*
Blassingame	*The Slave Community*
Williams, Chancellor	*The Destruction of Black Civilization*
Clark, R.T.	*Myth and Symbolism in Ancient Egypt*
DeCalo, Samuel	*Coups and Army Rule in Africa*

Ardrey, Robert	*African Genesis*
Poe, Richard	*Black Spark, White Fire*
Edgerton, Robert	*Africa's Armies*
Hancock, Graham	*The Sign and the Seal*
Osman, Ahmed	*Hebrew Pharaohs of Egypt*
Kramer, Samuel	*The Sumerians*
Jackson, John	*Introduction to African Civilization*
Morris, Donald	*Washing of the Spears*
Rodney, Walter	*How Europe Underdeveloped Africa*
Quirke, Stephen	*The Cult of Ra*
Kitchen, K.A.	*The Third Intermediate Period in Egypt*
Edgerton, Robert	*Hidden Heroism*